The Ultimate
JAPANESE NOODLES
COOKBOOK

Amazing Soba, Ramen, Udon, Hot Pot and Japanese Pasta Recipes!

Masahiro Kasahara

TUTTLE Publishing

Tokyo | Rutland, Vermont | Singapore

Contents

A Word from the Author

I just can't stop talking about cooking noodles! They're an indispensable part of washoku (or traditional Japanese cuisine). For example, if we're talking about soba noodles, my preference is for the classics like tsukimi (moon-gazing) soba, where the moon (tsuki) is represented by an egg yolk. I'm also a fan of tanuki (raccoon dog) soba, using tempura batter bits that are traditional to the Kanto region of Japan where I'm from. My favorite ramen is one with a light soy-sauce-flavored broth, which are like the ones we used to call "Chinese soba"when I was a child. As for udon, I still have fond memories of the stir-fried yakiudon I used to make for my lunch after morning classes were done on Saturdays.

As an adult, I started to go to my favorite soba restaurants on my own regularly. I also used to dash into ramen joints to take a break during working hours to grab a quick bowl of noodles, although the noodles were never enough to satiate me, so I'd get some fried rice on the side too. All in all, noodles are relaxed, easy food that help you feel relaxed and peaceful.

The best thing about noodles is that you can make them in a jiffy even when you're pressed for time. Although as a food professional I'd love for everyone to enjoy cooking all the time, there are times when we all feel like we just can't be bothered to make something: too much effort. That's when you just need to bring a pot of water to a boil, cook up some noodles, add a sauce or soup and toppings of your choice and have an easy, satisfying meal.

Whether it's Japanese noodles like udon, soba, or somen, Chinese noodles, Korean noodles, rice noodles that are eaten all over Asia or Italian pasta, there are noodle dishes from all over the world in so many variations.

In this book, I've arranged the recipes by the type of noodles I used that I think suit the flavors the best, but you can easily switch the noodles out as you like, and the dishes should still work well. After all, noodles give you so much freedom!

I'm the type of person who gets excited thinking about exactly how I'm going to be breaking up that beautiful egg yolk sitting on top of my tsukimi-soba even before I start. Nothing would make me happier than to share some of that noodly excitement with you.

—**Masahiro Kasahara**

How to Make Dashi Stock

INGREDIENTS

3-inch (7-cm/5 g) square piece kombu
1⅓ cups (15 g) bonito flakes
2 cups (500 ml) water

DIRECTIONS

Put the ingredients in a medium saucepan over high heat. When it comes to a boil, lower the heat and simmer for about 1 minute. Strain through a colander, pressing on the contents with the back of a spoon. Can be stored in the refrigerator up to 4 days.

How to Use This Book

- Standard measuring spoons are used. 1 teaspoon is 5 ml; 1 tablespoon is 15 ml.
- US cup measurements are used, with 1 cup rounded out to 240 ml.
- The original weight measurements are in grams. For the sake of simplicity, 1 ounce has been rounded out to 30 grams.
- Unless indicated otherwise, always start cooking on the stovetop with the heat set to medium.
- I have omitted basic instructions such as "wash and peel the vegetables" from the recipes for the sake of brevity. Please prep them as needed.
- Please be careful when handing hot oil or boiling water.
- Most of the ingredients used in this book can be found at a well-stocked supermarket. Otherwise you should be able to find them at a general Asian grocery store, or a Japanese grocery store. Feel free to substitute if you can't find something though, and have fun!

How to Interpret the Bowl Symbols

These bowl symbols are used in noodles plus soup recipes, and indicate the temperatures of each. You can vary these as you like, depending on the season and that day's weather.

Noodles: **Hot** Soup: **Hot**
Both the noodles and soup are served piping hot. For udon soup on cold days and ramen.

Noodles: **Cold** Soup: **Room Temp**
The noodles are served chilled, and the soup is served at room temperature. For noodle soups that are served with hot toppings or sides.

Noodles: **Cold** Soup: **Cold**
For noodle dishes where you want to fully savor the flavor and fragrance of the noodles themselves, such as cold soba.

Noodles: **Cold** Soup: **Hot**
Some chilled noodles are served with a hot soup or sauce to dip them in.

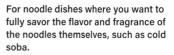

With Just This Sauce, Your Noodles Will Taste Amazing!

My Almighty, All-Purpose Mentsuyu Sauce

Let's start by making a basic mentsuyu or noodle sauce. Commercial mentsuyu in bottles is now widely available at Japanese grocery stores, but my version here is very good and very versatile. This is a non-concentrated version that can be used as is as a dipping sauce for cold soba noodles or cold somen noodles. Or if you dilute this with twice the amount of dashi stock, you can use it as a hot noodle soup, and if you dilute it with 3 times the amount of dashi stock it can be used as a pour-over sauce. This mentsuyu is very easy to make. Just put all the ingredients in a pan, bring to a boil and leave to cool in the pan. Then simply strain off the liquid, and it's done! I add equal amounts of dark (or regular) soy sauce and light or usukuchi soy sauce to my formula. This means that the sauce is well seasoned, since light soy sauce is saltier than dark, yet still has excellent depth of flavor and a beautiful color too. This mentsuyu keeps well, so you can make it in quantity and have it stored in advance. (Refer to the chart on the next page for making larger amounts.)

Use as a dipping sauce | Dilute with dashi to use as soup | Pour over noodles

SERVES 2

2-inch (5-cm) square piece dried konbu seaweed for dashi (about 1/6 oz or 5g)

½ oz (15 g) shaved katsuobushi (fermented and dried skipjack tuna)

1/6 oz (5 g) iriko or dried anchovies for making dashi

2 tablespoons dark soy sauce

2 tablespoons light soy sauce

4 tablespoons mirin

1 tablespoon sugar

1¼ cups (300 ml) water

1. PUT ALL THE INGREDIENTS IN A PAN

Put all the ingredients in a pan. Spread out each piece of the katsuobushi flakes so that they will yield as much flavor as possible.

3. TAKE THE PAN OFF THE HEAT

Turn the heat off, and leave the pan to cool.

2. SIMMER

Start heating over medium heat. When the liquid comes to a boil, turn the heat down low, and simmer for another 5 minutes or so.

4. STRAIN WITH A COLANDER

Line a colander with paper towels and strain the liquid. Press down on the contents with the back of a ladle to extract as much liquid as possible.

ALL-PURPOSE MENTSUYU SAUCE
(makes about 1¼ cups/300 ml)

To keep the sauce, transfer to a clean container and refrigerate for up to 5 days. The sauce can be used to flavor chicken-and-egg rice bowls (oyakodon), pork cutlet rice bowls (katsudon) and a lot more. You can use it as a sauce on cold tofu or blanched vegetables.

TO MAKE LARGER AMOUNTS

Easy to make and so delicious!

Ingredient	4 servings	6 servings
Konbu seaweed	4 inch (10 cm) square	6 inch (15 cm)
Katsuobushi	1 oz (30 g)	1½ oz (45 g)
Iriko	⅓ oz (10 g)	½ oz (15 g)
Dark soy sauce	¼ cup (60 ml)	⅓ cup (90 ml)
Light soy sauce	¼ cup (60 ml)	⅓ cup (90 ml)
Mirin	½ cup (120 ml)	¾ cup (180 ml)
Sugar	2 tablespoons	2 tablespoons
Water	2½ cups (600 ml)	3⅞ cups (900ml)

Basic Rules for Noodle Success

Anyone can successfully cook noodle dishes by remembering just a few key points. Keep these 3 factors in mind to make any noodle recipe you'd like to!

Don't forget that the noodles are the stars

Let's take the example of a bowl of ramen with lots of bean sprouts and corn in it. When you want to dive into a bowl of noodle soup, if the other elements are too present, they get in the way. They also make the noodles harder to eat. Never forget that in a noodle dish, the noodles are the stars. Sides or toppings with crunchy texture, such as as bamboo shoots, need to be cut up small, so they harmonize well with the noodles. Try grating carrots to make them easier to eat (see page 66).

Cook the noodles in plenty of boiling water

This is very basic, but very important. When cooking noodles, bring plenty of water to a rolling boil in a large pan, so that the noodles stay separate as they cook. If there's an inadequate amount of water, or if there are too many noodles to fit properly in the pan, the noodles won't cook properly. When cooking pasta, the basic rule is to add plenty of salt—1% of the weight of the boiling water—to the pan. Or improvise. Always be sure to drain the noodles well, or the sauce or soup may end up too runny or thin.

Noodles can be paired with any number of toppings or side dishes

Most noodles have a wheat flour base, so they go well with meat, seafood, vegetables, eggs, even fruits like citrus. The recipes in this book that are based on udon, soba and somen noodles all taste great if you switch one type for theother. Never think "I don't have enough ingredients so I can't make this." Just be flexible and work with what you have on hand, coming up with your own favorite taste combinations.

Chapter One

MY FAVORITE UDON RECIPES

When I was a child, "noodles" meant udon to me. Since both my parents worked outside the home, we often had a simple breakfast of udon noodles cooked in the leftover miso soup from the night before. No wonder it's a favorite with both children and adults.

All About Udon

Although there are all kinds of udon, such as precooked udon and dried udon, frozen udon is the best. Udon freezing technology has advanced a lot recently, and nowadays freshly cooked udon is flash frozen, so that you only need to cook it for about a minute to enjoy chewy, smooth and bouncy udon noodles. They are truly perfect for people who are busy. The one thing to pay attention to is to always cook the frozen udon in lots of boiling water. This is the iron rule for any kind of noodle, but for frozen udon in particular, because it is frozen and low in temperature, if you don't have plenty of hot water the temperature will go down too fast.

HOW TO BOIL UDON

Bring plenty of water to a boil in a big pan. Add the frozen udon noodles and cook them while separating the noodles with cooking chopsticks. Drain very well. If you are using them in a chilled udon dish, rinse the cooked noodles under cold running water, and drain well again. Frozen udon noodles are already cooked, so they are fine as long as they are heated through.

TIP BY KASAHARA

Always have cornstarch or potato starch dissolved in water handy for thickening sauces I often use cornstarch or potato starch dissolved in water in udon recipes. Not only does this thicken sauces and soups so that the flavors coat the noodles better, it also helps to retain the heat of the sauce or soup, so the dish is piping hot when you tuck into it. The usual ratio for mixing starch and water is 1 to 1, but I often use a ratio of 1 to 1.5, such as 1 tablespoon of starch to 1.5 tablespoon of water. By adding this little by little the the sauce or soup, you are much less likely to create lumps. Starch water can be made in advance and stored in the refrigerator for 3 to 4 days, so it's a good idea to have some made and in stock. Mix it up well before you use it, since the starch tends to settle in the bottom of the container.

THE UDON I USED FOR THIS BOOK

I used frozen udon that comes in 2 packs of 120 grams (about 4 ounces) each. They are the thick, smooth and chewy Sanuki udon type, which originally comes from Kagawa prefecture. Although they can be defrosted in their packets in the microwave too, I highly recommend that you boil them in lots of water as described. They only take a moment to cook that way too—so fast!

Noodles: **Cold**
Soup: **Room Temp**

Pork Shabu Shabu Udon

Pork shabu shabu, thin slices of pork quickly cooked in a broth, is a staple of summer in Japan. Here I have used them in a cold udon dish. The crispy texture of the myoga ginger buds is very refreshing. If you can't find myoga ginger buds, try using fresh ginger shoots or very young shredded ginger root instead. Mix everything well before eating. The sesame oil adds an appetizing fragrance to this dish.

SERVES 2

2 portions frozen udon noodles
5 oz (150 g) very thinly slicked pork for shabu shabu
3 myoga ginger buds, available at well-stocked Japanese grocery stores
A large pinch of salt
1 teaspoon sesame oil

FOR THE SOUP

⅔ cup (150 ml) All-Purpose Mentsuyu Sauce (page 6)
⅔ cup (150 ml) Dashi Stock (page 5)

DIRECTIONS

1. Slice the myoga ginger buds thinly and place in a bowl of cold water to crisp up. Combine the soup ingredients.

2. Bring a pan of water to a boil. Add the salt and turn off the heat. Take each slice of pork in between chopsticks, spread out into a single sheet, and wave it around briefly in the hot water until it's cooked. Take out the meat when it changes color, and drain in a colander.

3. Cook the udon noodles in plenty of boiling water, and drain. Rinse under running cold water to cool, and drain again. Arrange in bowls and pour the soup over them. Top with the cooked pork slices and drained shredded myoga ginger. Swirl on some sesame oil before serving.

Curry Udon Noodle Soup

This is the type of curry udon noodle bowl that's served at a traditional washo Japanese (washoku) restaurant. It's so simple, with just the addition of thinly sliced pork and onions, which are sautéed in butter to add flavor and richness. Mentsuyu sauce is used to add a traditional Japanese flavor. Eaten piping hot while blowing on the noodles to cool them down, they're irresistable.

2 portions frozen udon noodles, 4 oz (120 g) each
½ medium onion
5 oz (150 g) thinly sliced pork
1⅓ tablespoons (20 g) butter
1 tablespoon curry powder
1 teaspoon of cornstarch or potato starch dissolved in 1 tablespoon cold water
Chopped scallions, to serve

FOR THE SOUP
1 cup (240ml) All-Purpose Mentsuyu Sauce (page 6)
1½ cups (360 ml) Dashi Stock (page 5)

DIRECTIONS

1. Slice the onion thinly. Cut the pork into bite-sized pieces if necessary.
2. Melt the butter in a frying pan and sauté the onion and pork. When the meat changes color, sprinkle in the curry powder and sauté until it's fragrant.
3. Add the Soup ingredients and bring to a boil. Add the starch water and bring to a boil again while stirring to thicken the Soup a little.
4. Cook the udon noodles in plenty of boiling water, and drain well. Put the noodles in a bowl, pour over the Soup from Step 3 and top with the scallions.

TIPS

Add the thickening starch water a little at a time

When adding cornstarch or potato starch water to a soup or sauce to thicken it, scoop up a bit of the soup into a ladle and add the thickener to the ladle rather than to the main soup. Then stir it in slowly. If you try to add the thickener all at once, it may form lumps.

Noodles: **Hot**
Soup: **Hot**

The Stir-Fried Yaki Udon from My Childhood

This is the yaki udon or stir-fried udon noodle dish I used to make for myself when I was in school. Thick, chewy udon noodles are delicious when they're cooked this way. The meat here has to be pork! Add a ton of vegetables, top with a fried egg, and break the yolk to use as a runny sauce as you eat.

SERVES 2

2 portions frozen udon noodles, 4 oz (120 g) each
1 large cabbage leaf
⅓ medium carrot
1 medium green bell pepper
2 tablespoons vegetable oil
4 oz (120 g) thinly sliced pork
A pinch of salt
Black pepper, to taste
2 eggs
Large handful katsuobushi flakes
1 tablespoon or more beni-shoga (red pickled ginger)

FOR THE SAUCE

⅞ cup (200ml) All-Purpose Mentsuyu Sauce (page 6)
1 tablespoon mirin
1 tablespoon sake
1 tablespoon dark soy sauce

DIRECTIONS

1. Cook the udon noodles in plenty of boiling water, and drain well. Rinse under cold running water, and drain well again.
2. Chop up the cabbage roughly. Cut the carrot into matchsticks, and the bell pepper into thin slices. Combine the Sauce ingredients in a bowl.
3. Heat up 1 tablespoon of vegetable oil in a frying pan and stir fry the pork. When the pork has changed color, add the vegetables and salt and keep stir frying.
4. When the carrot is cooked through, add the udon noodles and stir fry. Add the sauce ingredients and black pepper.
5. In a separate small frying pan, add the remaining 1 tablespoon of vegetable oil, break in the eggs and sprinkle with a little salt to make 2 sunny-side-up fried eggs. When the whites have cooked through, add 1 tablespoon of water to the frying pan, cover with a lid and cook for 30 seconds. Turn off the heat.
6. Transfer the noodles to 2 plates, top with an egg each, as well as the katsuobushi flakes and red pickled ginger.

TIPS

My way of making yaki udon is to add in the sauce as I stir fry.

By adding plenty of sauce, bringing it to a boil and letting it cook down, the noodles absorb lots of flavor and become plump and juicy. The vegetables become deliciously crisp-tender too, and the meat is succulent.

Sizzling Hot Chicken and Mushroom Udon

This simple dish of piping hot noodles is made by simply adding udon noodles and mentsuyu to a heavy pot, ideally one that's cast iron or earthenware, and heating it up. It's a perfect quick meal when you are short on time, and makes a great late night snack too. I really recommend it on cold days, since it warms you right up. You can add any additional ingredients you like to this.

SERVES 2

2 portions frozen udon noodles, 4 oz (120 g) each
4 oz (120 g) boneless dark chicken meat or chicken thigh meat
1 large green onion or ⅓ small leek
2 fresh shiitake mushrooms
1 small bunch komatsuna greens or spinach leaves
2 rice cakes (mochi)
2 eggs

FOR THE SOUP
1 cup (240ml) All-Purpose Mentsuyu Sauce (page 6)
1½ cups (360 ml) Dashi Stock (page 5)

DIRECTIONS

1. Cook the udon noodles in plenty of boiling water, and drain well.
2. Cut up the chicken into bite-sized pieces. Slice the green onion or leek into thin diagonal slices.Cut the shiitake mushrooms in half.
3. Cut up the komatsuna greens or spinach roughly and put into a bowl of cold water. Drain well and squeeze out. Cut into 2 inch (5 cm) pieces.
4. Grill the mochi rice cakes until puffy and tender in a toaster oven.
5. Put the cooked udon noodles and the Soup ingredients in a pan, and top with the chicken, green onion or leek and shiitake mushrooms. Turn on the heat and bring to a boil, then lower the heat to a simmer. Add the greens and the grilled mochi rice cakes. Break the eggs on top, and simmer until the eggs are cooked to your desired degree of doneness. Serve piping hot.

TIPS

Chicken is a must for nabeyaki udon, as are grilled mochi rice cakes and eggs. Don't get too hung up on what kind of vegetables to add—use up what you have in the refrigerator. Try adding slices of fish cakes or sprinkling on some seven-spice mix.

Udon Smothered in Meat Sauce Hot and Cold Jaa Jaa Udon

"Jaa jaa" is an onomatopoeic phrase that expresses the contrast between the hot sauce and the cold noodles in this dish. Rich, sizzling meat sauce is served on top of chilled udon noodles in this fun and filling study in contrasts. Use thick udon noodles, which pair better with the rich meat sauce, and don't cut up the vegetables too small either.

SERVES 2

2 portions frozen udon noodles, 4 oz (120 g) each
5 oz (150 g) ground mixed pork and beef, or ground beef
2 oz (60 g) canned or vacuum cooked bamboo shoots
¼ onion
2 fresh shiitake mushrooms
1 tablespoon sesame oil
2 tablespoons starch water, for thickening (page 10)
1 small or ½ large cucumber
1 green onion
½ medium tomato
2 poached eggs

FOR THE SAUCE

1 teaspoon chicken bouillon dissolved in 1⅔ cups (400 ml) water
3 tablespoons tian mian jiang (Chinese sweet bean paste)
1 tablespoon soy sauce
½ teaspoon grated garlic
½ teaspoon grated ginger

DIRECTIONS

1. Cut the bamboo shoot into ⅓ inch (1 cm) dice. Chop the onion and shiitake mushrooms roughly. Combine the Sauce ingredients.
2. Heat the sesame oil in a frying pan and stir fry the ground meat and cut-up vegetables from Step 1 over medium heat.
3. When the meat changes color, add the combined sauce ingredients and bring to a boil Add the cornstarch dissolved in water and mix quickly to thicken the sauce.
4. Cut the cucumber and green onion into thin matchsticks, and slice the tomato into rounds.
5. Cook the udon noodles in plenty of boiling water until loosened, and drain well. Rinse under cold running water, and drain well again. Arrange on a plate and pour the Step 3 Sauce over it. Top with the Step 4 vegetables and poached eggs to serve.

TIPS

Let the flavors build as the noodles absorb the sauce

Here there are so many elements that blend so beautifully, hot and cold, hearty meat sauce with light and crunchy vegetables. The spongy udon noodles serve as the perfect bed or platform for these contrasting tastes.

Noodles: **Hot**
Soup: **Hot**

Classic Beef Udon

Meat-topped udon is usually made with pork in the Kanto region where I live, but here I've used beef for a Kansai region version. The key to this dish is the beef and leek that are cooked together in the savory-sweet mentsuyu; it's a winning combination. Try the beef-leek mixture with egg as a topping for a beef bowl as well!

SERVES 2

2 portions frozen udon noodles,
    4 oz (120 g) each
6 oz (200 g) thinly sliced beef
½ cup (100 ml) All-Purpose
    Mentsuyu Sauce (page 6)
½ leek
3 sprigs mitsuba or flat-leaf
    parsley

FOR THE SOUP
1 cup (240ml) All-Purpose
    Mentsuyu Sauce (page 6)
1½ cups (360 ml) Dashi Stock
    (page 5)

DIRECTIONS

1. Blanch the beef quickly in boiling water and drain in a colander. Put the sauce in a small pan, and add the beef. Cook until there is little liquid left in the pan.
2. Cut the leek into ⅓ inch (1 cm) long diagonal slices, and chop up the mitsuba or parsley roughly.
3. Put the leek in the pan with the Soup ingredients and bring to a boil.
4. Cook the udon noodles in plenty of boiling water, and drain. Put into a bowl, and ladle in the Step 3 Soup. Top with the beef mixture, and garnish with the mitsuba or parsley leaves.

TIPS

Flavor the beef well
Simmer it with the mentsuyu sauce to give it lots of flavor. Slower cooking also helps to tenderize it.

Noodles: **Hot**
Soup: **Hot**

Tomato, Cheese and Bacon Udon

Tomatoes in oden, a classic fish-cake stew, were all the rage at one time. Tomatoes are really packed with umami and are a great supplement to dashi stock. Here I've combined tomatoes with cheese and bacon, which go so well together. You can use sausage instead of bacon if you wish.

SERVES 2

2 portions frozen udon noodles,
    4 oz (120 g) each
1 medium tomato
3 slices bacon
1 tablespoon grated cheese
Coarsely ground black pepper,
    to taste

FOR THE SOUP

1 cup (240ml) All-Purpose
    Mentsuyu Sauce (page 6)
1½ cups (360 ml) Dashi Stock
    (page 5)

DIRECTIONS

1. Cut the tomato up roughly, and cut the bacon into ⅓ inch (1 cm) dice.
2. Put the bacon, tomato and Soup ingredients in a pan and bring to a boil.
3. Cook the udon noodles in plenty of boiling water, and drain. Put into bowls and ladle in the Soup from Step 2. Top with grated cheese and black pepper.

TIPS

Use tomatoes for their umami

By simply simmering tomatoes, bacon and mentsuyu together, you can make an exceptionally delicious udon soup. The acids in the tomato and the umami in the bacon combine to create an unbeatable combination that suggests a savory Italian amatriciana.

Noodles: **Cold**
Soup: **Cold**

Vinegared Seaweed and Cucumber Udon

There's a classic washoku dish called mozuku rice bowl. This is an udon variation that I came up with, intergrating packets of mozuku seaweeed in vinegar sauce. This is so refreshing to eat, even on the hottest summer day. Give it a try!

SERVES 2

2 portions frozen udon noodles,
   4 oz (120 g) each
4 packs mozuku seaweed in
   vinegar sauce (available at
   Japanese grocery stores)
1 small or ½ large cucumber
½ teaspoon salt
1 teaspoon grated ginger
1 tablespoon toasted sesame
   seeds

FOR THE SOUP
⅔ cup (150 ml) All-Purpose
   Mentsuyu Sauce (page 6)
⅔ cup (150 ml) Dashi Stock
   (page 5)

DIRECTIONS

1. Put the mozuku seaweed in vinegar sauce and the Soup ingredients in a bowl and combine. Chill in the refrigerator.
2. Slice the cucumber thinly and sprinkle with the salt. Squeeze with your hands to rub the salt in, and then squeeze tightly to eliminate any extra moisture.
3. Cook the udon noodles in plenty of boiling water, and drain. Rinse under running cold water to cool, and drain again. Arrange in bowls and top with the Step 1 mixture.
4. Add the cucumber, ginger and sesame seeds and serve.

Creamy Egg Sauce Udon

Combine the eggs with the fresh cream beforehand to make a creamy custard-like mixture. Oyster sauce is used here instead of the usual soy sauce for a twist. You'll be pleasantly surprised by the amazingly smooth texture.

SERVES 2

2 portions frozen udon noodles,
    4 oz (120 g) each
3 eggs
2 scallions, finely minced

THE CUSTARD MIXTURE
1 tablespoon heavy cream
1 teaspoon sesame oil
1 teaspoon oyster sauce
2 pinches salt

DIRECTIONS

1. Break the eggs into a heatproof bowl and mix with the Custard Mixture ingredients. Place the bowl on top of a pan of hot water to use as a double boiler, and whip the mixture with a whisk until creamy and fluffy.
2. Cook the udon noodles in plenty of boiling water, and drain. Place into bowls and top with the egg mixture. Sprinkle with green scallions and serve.

TIPS

Use boiling water in a double boiler
When cooking the eggs over hot water, make sure the water is boiling hot so the eggs become properly fluffy and creamy. Keep whisking until they're the consistency you want.

Fluffy Egg Drop Udon

Thickened creamy soup is combined with fluffy, elegant scrambled eggs in this classic udon dish. By thickening the soup first before adding the eggs a little at a time, they'll turn out fluffy and soft. The fragrance of the mitsuba or parsley adds a nice accent.

SERVES 2

2 portions frozen udon noodles, 4 oz (120 g) each
1 green onion
3 sprigs mitsuba or flat-leaf parsley
1 tablespoon starch water (page 10)
2 eggs

FOR THE SOUP
1 cup (240ml) All-Purpose Mentsuyu Sauce (page 6)
1½ cups (360 ml) Dashi Stock (page 5)

DIRECTIONS

1. Slice the green onion thinly diagonally. Cut the leaves off the mitsuba sprigs or parsley, and chop the stems into 1-inch (2.5-cm) pieces.
2. Put the Soup ingredients into a pan and bring to a boil. Add the starch water and mix to thicken the Soup. Add the sliced green onion and boil briefly.
3. Break the eggs into a bowl and mix well. Add to the hot Soup from Step 2 using a ladle a little at a time.
4. Cook the udon noodles and drain. Place into bowls, pour the Soup over them. Top with the mitsuba or parsley leaves.

TIPS

Add the egg to the thickened soup

After adding the eggs, don't stir them. Just gently swirl the pan, and they'll turn out soft and fluffy.

Chapter Two

SOBA IS SO GOOD

It took me a while but eventually, in adulthood, I became a soba fan. It goes down so well. Sometimes I go out to a soba joint to enjoy the noodles all on my own. Of all the noodle types, only soba has a definite "season." Maybe I'm drawn to that aspect of it, which is quintessentially Japanese, while still so adaptable to other cuisines.

All About Soba

For making at home, dried soba noodles are best!

I like handmade fresh soba noodles so much that I actually opened a fresh soba noodle restaurant (to be precise, I found a great soba maker and hired him). Freshly made soba noodles are great, but you may want to enjoy them at a restaurant rather than at home. For soba at home, dried noodles are much easier and harder to mess up. I recommend choosing the ones with the least number of ingredients. Another thing to factor in is to try to pick noodles that come from a region that's known for having good soba, such as Nagano prefecture (also called Shinshu). This is the best way to enjoy the flavor (and fragrance!) of soba, but delicious options are available anywhere, just look around for the best offerings.

THE SOBA I USED IN THIS BOOK

I used simple soba, which has 120 grams (4 ounces) of dried noodles per bundle. It contains soba (buckwheat) flour, wheat flour and salt. If you look at the noodles closely, they have tiny specks—that's the buckwheat hull. The noodles are on the thick side and are spongy and chewy; the more you savor them, the more of the flavor of the buckwheat fills your mouth. Soba also cooks quite quickly, taking only about about 4 minutes.

HOW TO COOK SOBA NOODLES

Bring plenty of water to a boil. Add the soba noodles.

Mix the noodles up lightly with long cooking chopsticks, and cook them in lots of boiling water for 4 minutes. If it looks like the water is going to boil over, turn the heat down.

Rinse the noodles under lots of cold running water. Do it quickly and efficiently to preserve their integrity. In summer, use ice water instead to cool the noodles down fast.

Noodles: **Cold**
Soup: **Cold**

Watercress and Grated Daikon Pour-Over Soba

This is a variation of one of our restaurant's most popular dishes. Here I've added shirasu, salted and boiled whitefish, for added richness and flavor and use just the tender leaves of the watercress, since they blend better with the noodles and are easier to eat. You can substitute boiled octopus for the shirasu or thin deep-fried tofu for a meatless option.

SERVES 2

2 bundles dried soba noodles,
    4 oz (120 g) each
1 standard bunch watercress
2 oz (60 g) shirasu, available
    at Japanese grocery stores
    in the refrigerated or frozen
    section

FOR THE SOUP
⅔ cup (150ml) All-Purpose
    Mentsuyu Sauce (page 6)
⅔ cup (150ml) Dashi Stock
    (page 5)

DIRECTIONS

1. Remove the leaves of the watercress from the stems.
2. Boil the soba noodles in plenty of water, drain and rinse under cold running water. Drain well again. Arrange on a soup plate or in a flat bowl.
3. Chill the Soup and pour over the noodles. Arrange the shirasu and watercress leaves on top.

TIPS

The leftover watercress stems from this recipe are used as garnish for other dishes. Chop it up finely and mix it with grated daikon radish, and it becomes a perfect accompaniment to sashimi or meat dishes.

Pork and Leek Soba

Nanban soba is usually made with duck, but here I've used nutrient-packed pork instead. A Nanban soba means it has leeks in it. The umami of the cooked pork and the fragrance of the leek combine to create a deeply flavored, complex dipping sauce.

SERVES 2

2 bundles dried soba noodles -
    4 oz (120 g) x 2
3⅓ oz (100 g) thinly sliced pork
    belly
½ thin leek (Japanese or Asian
    leek preferred), or a thick
    green onion
3 sprigs mitsuba or flat-leaf
    parsley
A little fresh yuzu or lemon zest

FOR THE SOUP
1 cup plus ½ tablespoon
    (250ml) All-Purpose
    Mentsuyu Sauce (page 6)
1 cup (225 ml) Dashi Stock
    (page 5)

Vegetable oil, for cooking

DIRECTIONS

1. Cut up the pork into easy to eat pieces. Slice the leek into 1 inch (2.5 cm) long pieces, and the mitsuba or parsley sprigs into slightly shorter pieces.
2. Heat up the vegetable oil in a frying pan and put in the pork and leek. Stir fry until the meat changes color, then add the soup ingredients and bring to a boil.
3. Boil the soba noodles in plenty of boiling water, drain and rinse under cold running water. Drain well again. Arrange on plates or flat sieves.
4. Put the sauce with the pork and vegetables in other bowls, and top with the mitsuba and yuzu peel. Eat by dipping the noodles in the sauce.

TIPS

Be sure to brown both the pork and leeks very well

The delicious fat that is rendered from the pork becomes the umami of the dipping sauce. Make the leeks fragrant by browning them well. You can do this all at the same time in the frying pan.

Noodles: **Cold**
Soup: **Hot**

Hinomaru Soba

Hinomaru refers to the red circle on the white background of the Japanese flag, which the red plum and white yam in this dish resemble. The key to this dish is the crushed nagaimo mountain yam. Instead of grating it, as is usually the case, by crushing and roughly chopping it, a unique texture is created. Serve these noodles with lots of chilled soup, and mix them with the unique textures of the nagaimo.

SERVES 2

2 bundles dried soba noodles, 4 oz (120 g) each
One 3-inch (7-cm) piece yam or nagaimo yam, available at Asian grocery stores
A pinch salt
2 umeboshi salt-preserved ume fruit, available at Japanese grocery stores
5 leaves green shiso
Wasabi paste, to taste

FOR THE SOUP
⅔ cup (150ml) All-Purpose Mentsuyu Sauce (page 6)
⅔ cup (150ml) Dashi Stock (page 5)

DIRECTIONS

1. Peel the nagaimo yam. Bash it with the blunt edge of your knife: try to achieve a texture that's half chopped and half ground into a slimy texture. Sprinkle with a pinch of salt and mix lightly in a bowl.
2. Remove the pits from the umeboshi. Finely shred the green shiso leaves.
3. Boil the soba noodles in plenty of boiling water, drain and rinse under cold running water. Drain well again. Arrange on a soup plate or in a flat bowl.
4. Top the noodles with the crushed nagaimo yam and the umeboshi. Arrange the shiso and wasabi paste on top.
5. Serve the well-chilled Soup in a separate bowl, and pour it over the noodles just before eating.

Noodles: **Cold**
Soup: **Cold**

Chilled Crispy Tofu and Grated Daikon Soba

Kitsune soba is usually served warm with simmered kitsune, a piece of deep-fried tofu. But in this version, the kitsune has been panfried until crispy on the outside and soft and puffy on the inside, to provide a nice texture and temperature contrast with the cold noodles. Grated daikon radish and spicy radish sprouts make these noodles even more refreshing.

SERVES 2

- 2 bundles dried soba noodles, 4 oz (120 g) each
- 3-inch (7-cm) piece daikon radish
- 2 pieces aburaage (flat deep-fried tofu, available at Japanese grocery stores)
- ½ packet radish sprouts, about 2 oz (60 g)
- 1⅓ cups (300ml) All-Purpose Mentsuyu Sauce (page 6)

DIRECTIONS

1. Grate the daikon radish and drain off the excess moisture in a colander.
2. Heat up a frying pan, and fry the aburaage without adding any oil, by pressing the pieces firmly against the bottom of the pan until they've browned. Repeat on the other side. Take out of the pan, and when they've cooled enough to handle, cut into ½ inch (1 cm) wide strips.
3. Boil the soba noodles in plenty of water, drain and rinse under cold running water. Drain well again. Arrange on a soup plate or in a flat bowl.
4. Top the noodles with the aburaage, grated daikon radish and the radish sprouts. Serve the well-chilled mentsuyu in a separate bowl, and eat the noodles while dipping them in the mentsuyu.

Noodles: **Cold**
Soup: **Cold**

Addictive Natto and Tofu Soba

I love natto—the sticky fermented soy bean condiment—although I do realize it's an acquired taste. Here I've combined them with silken tofu to make this a "bean fest" of a meal. The stickiness of the natto combines with the mentsuyu and tofu to create a soft-textured, gentle sauce. Even if you're skeptical about natto, give this a try. It just might make you into a convert.

SERVES 2

2 bundles dried soba noodles,
    4 oz (120 g) each
¼ block (about 3½ oz/100 g)
    silken tofu
2 packets (about 1⅔ oz/50 g
    each) natto
Minced scallions, to taste
Shredded nori seaweed, to taste

SAUCE A
The sauce and mustard packets
    that come with the natto
2 tablespoons All-Purpose
    Mentsuyu Sauce (page 6)

SAUCE B
⅔ cup (150ml) All-Purpose
    Mentsuyu Sauce (page 6)
⅔ cup (150ml) Dashi Stock
    (page 5)

DIRECTIONS

1. Wrap the tofu with paper towels and put a weight on it. Leave it to drain for about 20 minutes to drain off the excess water.
2. Crumble the tofu into a bowl. Add the natto and the Sauce A ingredients, and mix well.
3. Boil the soba noodles in plenty of water, drain and rinse under cold running water. Drain well again. Arrange on a soup plate or in a flat bowl.
4. Top the noodles with well-chilled Sauce B, the natto-tofu mixture, chopped scallions and shredded nori seaweed.

Noodles: **Hot**
Soup: **Hot**

Simple Nori Seaweed and Egg Soba

I love "tsukimi soba" or moon-watching soba. A single egg is dropped on top of hot soba noodles, and when hot dashi stock is poured over it, the egg white sets nicely, making the yolk look like the full moon in the night sky. I love this way of preparing a simple soba. In this version, I've also added some nori seaweed, turning it into a nori-tama (or nori and egg) soba.

SERVES 2

2 bundles dried soba noodles,
    4 oz (120 g) each
2 sheets of toasted nori sea-
    weed, about 8 x 7 inches
    (20 x 18 cm)
2 eggs

FOR THE SOUP
1 cup (240ml) All-Purpose
    Mentsuyu Sauce (page 6)
1½ cups (360 ml) Dashi Stock
    (page 5)

DIRECTIONS

1. Cut each sheet of nori into eighths.
2. Boil the soba noodles in plenty of boiling water, drain well and arrange in bowls.
3. Break an egg into the center of each bowl of noodles. Heat the Soup and ladle it over the noodles, serving with the nori.

Noodles: **Cold**
Soup: **Cold**

Tuna Salad Soba

Here's a summery spin on noodle salad or the classic macaroni tuna salad enjoyed at picnics and seasonal gatherings. The salty, soy-sauce-flavored tuna salad couched on a bed of soba offers a tasty alternative. The mentsuyu-based sauce works great as a general salad dressing as well.

SERVES 2

2 bundles dried soba noodles
½ cucumber, peeled
2 scallions or green onions
1 can (5 oz/140 g) tuna, drained
1 medium tomato
3 sprigs flat-leaf parsley
4 pieces green-leaf lettuce

SAUCE A
3 tablespoons mayonnaise
1 teaspoon mirin
1 teaspoon soy sauce

SAUCE B
⅔ cup (150ml) All-Purpose
   Mentsuyu Sauce (page 6)
⅔ cup (150ml) Dashi Stock
   (page 5)
1 tablespoon sesame oil
2 tablespoons rice vinegar

DIRECTIONS

1. Deseed and chop the cucumber. Slice the scallions. Add the well-drained tuna. Combine with the Sauce A ingredients
2. Cut the tomato in eighths and finely chop the mitsuba or parsley. Combine the Sauce B ingredients.
3. Boil the noodles in plenty of salted water. Rinse and drain.
4. Line the bowls with the lettuce leaves. Top with the tuna mixture, noodles and Sauce B. Place the tomato slices to the side and garnish with the fresh herbs.

Noodles: **Hot**
Soup: **Hot**

Refreshing Umeboshi and Wakame Seaweed Soba

This is soba at its simple, delicious best. The combination of the buckwheat noodles with the salty-sweet preserved plum and the seaweed makes for a comforting and satisfying dish. Whenever I catch a cold, I make a big pot of this and savor the flavors while slowly restoring my strength.

SERVES 2

2 bundles dried soba noodles,
    4 oz (120 g) each
Salted wakame seaweed,
    8 g (¼ oz)
4 thin slices kamaboko
4 umeboshi
1 teaspoon toasted sesame
    seeds

FOR THE SOUP
1 cup (240ml) All-Purpose
    Mentsuyu Sauce (page 6)
1½ cups (360 ml) Dashi Stock
    (page 5)

DIRECTIONS

1. Rinse the salt off the seaweed and soak in a little water. Squeeze out the excess liquid then roughly chop the seaweed.
2. Put the Soup ingredients in a pot and warm them up.
3. Boil the soba in a lot of salted water. Drain and rinse, then place the noodles on a plate or in a bowl. Add the Soup, two umeboshi for each serving and a sprinkle of the sesame seeds.

Noodles: **Hot**
Soup: **Hot**

My Favorite Scallion Tanuki Soba

The oil in the tempura batter bits is soaked up by the dashi stock, to make every comforting mouthful settle gently on a delicate stomach. By the way, this version is from Tokyo—so I think it might be called the "hoity toity" version? The Osaka version has a piece of aburaage (fried tofu) in it. Maybe you should concoct a version of your own!

SERVES 2

2 bundles dried soba noodles, 4 oz (120 g) each
4 scallions or green onions
3 tablespoons tenkasu (tempura batter bits, see Notes)

FOR THE SOUP
1 cup (240ml) All-Purpose Mentsuyu Sauce (page 6)
1½ cups (360 ml) Dashi Stock (page 5)

DIRECTIONS

1. Chop the green onions finely.
2. Boil the soba noodles in plenty of boiling water, drain and arrange on a soup plate or in a bowl.
3. Heat the Soup and pour over the noodles. Top with the green onions and tenkasu.

NOTES *Tenkasu are the bits of batter that fall off when you make tempura. You can buy tenkasu in small bags at Japanese grocery stores, or simply save some when you make tempura and store it in the freezer until ready to use.*

Noodles: **Cold**
Soup: **Cold**

Refreshingly Cold Citrus Soba

This cold noodle dish is popular at one of my restaurants. It looks wonderfully cooling to the eye, and the sudachi juice makes it very refreshing. With a light fragrance and acidity, this can be eaten even on the hottest summer day when you have no appetite. You'll want to drink up every drop of the broth.

SERVES 2

2 bundles dried soba noodles, 4 oz (120 g) each
6 sudachi citrus fruit (see Notes for substitutions)

FOR THE SOUP
1 cup (240ml) All-Purpose Mentsuyu Sauce (page 6)
1½ cups (360 ml) Dashi Stock (page 5)

NOTES *Sudachi is a citrus with lemon-orange hints. If you can't find it, substitute limes or Meyer lemons. You may have to adjust the amount of citrus used. Try mixing different types of citrus too, such as using pomelos or grapefruit along with lemons or limes; and remember the peel is eaten in this soup too.*

DIRECTIONS

1. Wash the sudachi citrus fruit well. Cut off the blossom end rather thickly, and slice the rest into thin rounds.
2. Squeeze out the juice from the cut-off blossom ends of the fruit and combine with the Soup ingredients in a bowl. Chill in the refrigerator.
3. Boil the soba noodles in plenty of water, drain and rinse under cold running water. Drain well again. Arrange in bowls, add the Soup, and top with the sudachi citrus slices to serve.

TIPS

Slice the citrus very thinly
Slice the citrus fruit very thinly, since the peel is also eaten in this refreshing soup. If you can get them very thin and evenly sliced, they'll be easier to eat too.

Yakumi Garnishes to Mix into Noodles

Yakumi are garnishes or condiments that add more than pretty color. They add flavor and texture, and some are purported to have health-giving qualities too. Here are some easy ways to make garnishes that you can mix in with noodles.

Colorful variations on grated daikon radish!

3-COLOR GRATED VEGETABLES—YELLOW

Combine one raw egg yolk (be sure it's pasteurized or farm-fresh), 4 tablespoons of grated daikon radish, a pinch of salt and a teaspoon of vegetable oil.

3-COLOR GRATED VEGETABLES—GREEN

Combine 5 minced green shiso leaves, 3 minces thin green scallions, 4 tablespoons grated daikon radish and a pinch of salt

3-COLOR GRATED VEGETABLES—RED

Combine 1 depitted and chopped umeboshi, 2 tablespoon minced shibazuke pickles, and 4 tablespoons grated daikon radish

The texture of celery is a nice accent!

KATSUOBUSHI AND CELERY

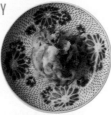

Combine ½ stalk celery, finely minced, 2 small bags of katsuobushi, 1 teaspoon soy sauce, 1 teaspoon mirin and 1 tablespoon vegetable oil.

A great marriage of fragrant ingredients

BLACK SESAME SEEDS AND SHUNGIKU

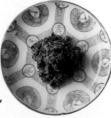

Blanch ½ bunch shungiku (garland chrysanthemum leaves, packed with umami, they're great on pasta) in salted water and squeeze out. Mince finely. Combine with 2 tablespoon ground black sesame seeds, 1 teaspoon soy sauce, 1 teaspoon mirin, and 1 teaspoon sesame oil.

A great condiment for pour-over noodles

GRILLED EGGPLANT RELISH

Grill 2 small Japanese eggplants until charred. Peel and chop up roughly. Combine with 1 teaspoon ginger root juice, 1 finely chopped myoga ginger bud, 3 thin green scallions, 1 teaspoon soy sauce, 1 teaspoon mirin and 1 tablespoon sesame oil.

Let the flavors meld in the fridge for 10 minutes

YAMAGATA-STYLE DASHI CONDIMENT

Combine 1 small Japanese cucumber cut into ½ inch (1 cm) dice, 1 small Japanese eggplant cut into ½ inch (1 cm) dice, 2 okra cut into ½ inch (1 cm) dice, 1 myoga ginger bud ½ inch (1 cm) dice, one 1 inch (2.5 cm) long piece nagaimo yam cut into ½ inch (1 cm) dice, 1 teaspoon salt, 1 tablespoon rice vinegar and 1 tablespoon vegetable oil.

Great on Chinese or Japanese style noodles!

LEEK AND SALT WITH BLACK PEPPER

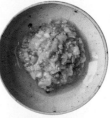

Chop up 1 thin leek finely. Combine with 1 teaspoon roasted white sesame seeds, ½ teaspoon coarsely ground black pepper, ½ teaspoon salt and 2 tablespoons sesame oil.

SALTED KONBU SEAWEED WITH GINGER

Combine 3 tablespoons finely minced shio-konbu (available at Japanese grocery stores), ⅔ tablespoon grated ginger, and 1 tablespoon vegetable oil.

Chapter Three

SOMEN IS NOT JUST FOR SUMMER!

Although somen noodles are commonly thought of as summer-time cold noodles in Japan, I think they are great year-round. They are ready in a jiffy, and go with vegetables, meat, fish or any ingredients. In the summer you just need some yakumi (condiments or garnishes—see page 38) and sauce, and you're ready to go! In the summer, enjoy them as warm nyuumen.

All About Somen

Hand-pulled somen noodles are the best, since they have good texture and don't overcook that easily.

If you can, choose somen noodles that have been hand-pulled rather than machine made. Hand-pulled noodles (called "tenobe") have better flavor and texture than machine-cut noodles, since they're thinner and subjected to more pressure. They're also rested for a longer time, which gives them more body and strength, so they don't turn limp as quickly when boiled. The key to good somen noodles is how you cook them. Bring a lot of water to a boil in a large pan, and cook the noodles over high heat while watching them so they don't boil over. As soon as they're done, drain and rinse them well under cold running water, then drain again. This firms up the texture of the noodles, but it's important to cook the noodles through so there's no uncooked raw part left.

THE SOMEN I USED IN THIS BOOK

I used hand-pulled (tenobe) somen, which come in 5 bundles of 50 grams each. They stand up to cooking, have nice body and a smooth texture. They also have good mouthfeel too. Although the cooking time for somen noodles depends on how thick they are, the ones I recommend are about 0.7 to 0.9 mm thick, and take 1.5 to 2 minutes to cook.

HOW TO COOK SOMEN NOODLES

   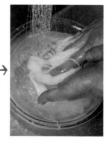

Bring plenty of water to a boil in a pan. Sprinkle in the somen and boil over high heat. Have the bundles of noodles undone and ready to go before you start cooking.

Stir the noodles gently. When the water comes back to a boil, adjust the heat so that it doesn't boil over. Cook the noodles for 1.5 to 2 minutes.

Be sure to taste a noodle to make sure it's not too al dente. If there are no crunchy or still overly firm strands, it's done.

Drain the noodles quickly into a colander, and rinse under cold running water to cool them quickly. Use both hands to rinse them, then drain very well.

Vegetable-Packed Somen "Jiro"

This is a tribute to the ever-popular Ramen Jiro restaurant chain. Chilled somen noodles are topped with boiled pork and lots of lightly cooked vegetables. This version is lower in fat and healthier than ramen, so add it to your regular weeknight rotation.

SERVES 2

3 bundles somen noodles,
　1⅔ oz (50 g) each
2 cabbage leaves
4-inch (5-cm) piece carrot
8 snow peas
A pinch salt
4 oz (120 g) thinly sliced pork
1 container (about 7 oz/200 g)
　bean sprouts
Ground black pepper, to taste

SAUCE A

3 tablespoons All-Purpose
　Mentsuyu Sauce (page 6)
2 tablespoons sesame oil
½ teaspoon grated garlic

SAUCE B

½ cup (120 ml) All-Purpose
　Mentsuyu Sauce (page 6)
½ cup (120 ml) Dashi Stock
　(page 5)

DIRECTIONS

1. Cut up the cabbage roughly. Cut the carrot into matchsticks. Take the strings off the snow peas.
2. Cook the somen noodles in plenty of boiling water and drain. Rinse under cold running water and drain again. Arrange in serving bowls.
3. Bring some water to a boil in a pan. Add a little salt to the water, and add the pork and all the vegetables including the bean sprouts to it. Cook until the pork changes color, and drain well. Mix with the Sauce A ingredients.
4. Pour Sauce B over the noodles, and top with the Step 3 ingredients. Finish with lots of black pepper.

Sichuan Eggplant Somen

Here I have combined a classic Sichuan Chinese dish, Mapo Eggplant, with classic Japanese somen. The juicy eggplant will fill your mouth with flavor. The meat sauce combines so well with the soft texture of the eggplant, that even on a sweltering hot summer's day, you'll be able to slurp this up with no problem!

SERVES 2

Three 1⅔ oz (50 g) bundle somen noodles, 5 oz (150 g) total
3⅓ oz (100 g) ground chicken
2 small Japanese or Asian eggplants
¼ onion
1 small piece ginger
1 teaspoon doubanjiang (spicy bean paste, available at Chinese or Asian grocery stores)
1 teaspoon sesame oil
1 tablespoon starch water (page 10)
2 tablespoons vegetable oil
Finely chopped scallions, to taste

FOR THE SOUP
1¼ cups (300 ml) chicken stock
1 tablespoon miso
1½ tablespoons soy sauce
1 tablespoon mirin
2 teaspoons sugar

DIRECTIONS

1. Cut the eggplants in half lengthwise and make fine diagonal cuts into the surface of the skins. Cut in half lengthwise again. Finely mince the onion and ginger. Combine the soup ingredients.
2. Heat up the vegetable oil in a frying pan, and stir fry the onion, ginger and ground meat. When it's starting to smell nice add the eggplant and continue stir frying.
3. When the eggplant has wilted, add the doubanjiang and continue stir frying. Add the soup ingredients and bring to a boil. Add the starch water and stir to thicken.
4. Cook the somen in plenty of boiling water and drain well. Rinse under cold running water, and drain well again. Sprinkle with the sesame oil.
5. Arrange the noodles in serving bowls, top with the Step 3 mixture, and sprinkle with the chopped scallions to serve.

TIPS

Make fine diagonal cuts into the eggplants

Eggplants have tough skins, so if you make small cuts into the skin they will cook easier and flavors will penetrate them better. They'll also look nicer.

Sea Bream and Sliced Mushroom Nyuumen

Nyuumen is somen served hot. This dish is perfect for festive occasions, which is when sea bream (called *tai*) is served in Japan. The fish is quickly blanched to get rid of any fishiness before it's simmered gently to a tender finish. The slightly sweet simmering sauce combines with the dashi for a delicious result. At our restaurant, we've made a similar dish using fugu (pufferfish) too.

SERVES 2

3 bundles somen noodles,
    1⅔ oz (50 g) each
2 sea bream filets, approximately 3 oz (90 g) each
2 fresh shiitake mushrooms
Sansho pepper sprigs, for
    garnish

FOR THE SAUCE
⅞ cup (200 ml) All-Purpose
    Mentsuyu Sauce (page 6)
3 tablespoons plus 1 teaspoon
    (50 ml) sake
1 teaspoon sugar

FOR THE SOUP
⅞ cup (200 ml) All-Purpose
    Mentsuyu Sauce (page 6)
1⅔ cups (400 ml) Dashi Stock
    (page 5)

DIRECTIONS

1. Dip the sea bream filets briefly in plenty of boiling water, then immediately put them into ice water to cool them. Drain well. (This procedure is called "frosting" the fish, and takes away their fishy odor.) Slice the shiitake mushrooms thinly.

2. Put the Sauce ingredients in a pan and bring to a boil. Add the fish filets and simmer. When the liquid has reduced to ⅓ of its original volume, turn off the heat, and leave the fish to cook in residual heat until it's cooled to room temperature.

3. Cook the somen noodles in plenty of boiling water and drain. Rinse under cold running water and drain again. Arrange on serving plates.

4. Heat up the Soup and pour over the noodles. Top with the fish from Step 2, and garnish with a sprig of sansho pepper, if you have it. If not, try dill.

TIPS

"Frost" the fish to remove any fishy odor

By "frosting" fresh fish (see Step 1) and putting it briefly in hot water, you can take away its fishy odor. Putting the fish in ice water directly afterward firms the flesh.

TIPS

Simmer fish to a nice finish

In order to have whole firm filets simmered in a sauce, it's important not to touch them while they're cooking. If it looks like the surface of the fish is drying out, spoon the cooking liquid over it. By cooking fish with shiitake mushrooms, the fish takes on their fragrance.

Noodles: **Hot**
Soup: **Hot**

Creamy Turnip and Enoki Mushroom Nyuumen

The key to this warming dish is to make sure the turnips retain some of their texture and don't get overcooked. Although I do love soft, almost mushy turnips myself, in this dish keeping some of the crunchy texture is key. The creamy dashi-based sauce surrounds the vegetables gently for a lovely flavor. The black pepper added at the end brings it all together.

SERVES 2

3 bundles somen noodles, 1⅔ oz (50 g) each
2 small Japanese turnips (available at Japanese grocery stores) or 4 baby turnips
2 packets enoki mushrooms, 3½ oz (100 g) each
2½ cups (600 ml) Dashi Stock (page 5)
1 tablespoon starch water (page 10)
Finely minced scallions, to taste
Ground black pepper, to taste

FOR THE SAUCE
3 tablespoons heavy cream
2 teaspoons usukuchi (light-colored) soy sauce
2 tablespoons mirin
1 teaspoon salt

DIRECTIONS

1 Cut the turnips into 12 wedges each (peel them first if the skins are tough). Cut the root ends off the enoki mushrooms, cut the rest in half and shred apart.

2. Put the vegetables in a pan with the dashi stock and bring to a boil. Lower the heat and simmer for 10 minutes.

3. Add the starch water and mix quickly to thicken the dashi. Add the Sauce ingredients, and heat. Turn off the heat just before it comes to a boil.

4. Cook the somen noodles in plenty of boiling water and drain. Rinse under cold running water and drain again. Pour the Step 3 mixture over the noodles in serving bowls. Top with the scallions and sprinkle on plenty of black pepper.

TIPS

Do not overheat heavy cream

Add the seasonings, such as mirin and soy sauce, to the cream before you add it to the pan. If you overcook cream, it may split, so you just need to heat it through gently.

TIPS

The turnip pieces shouldn't be too thick or too thin

Turnip cooks very quickly, so if you slice it too thinly it will fall apart. This time I've cut each turnip into 12 sections. The enoki mushrooms are cut to be about the same length as the turnips, to make them easier to cook.

Noodles: **Cold**
Soup: **Cold**

Poached Egg, Salmon Roe and Avocado Somen

Avocado mixed with soy sauce and wasabi go so well with the chilled mentsuyu. Making the soft-set poached eggs is a matter of timing, but shouldn't be too hard to master quickly. I've included instructions in Step 1. Make sure you mix everything up well before eating. This is guaranteed to be a new favorite!

SERVES 2

3 bundles somen noodles,
  1⅔ oz (50 g) each
2 soft-poached eggs
1 ripe avocado
1⅓ oz (40 g) ikura or salmon
  eggs marinated in soy sauce
  (available at Japanese grocery stores) or salmon caviar
Shredded nori seaweed, to
  taste

SAUCE A
1 teaspoon soy sauce
½ teaspoon wasabi paste
1 tablespoon vegetable oil

SAUCE B
½ cup (120 ml) All-Purpose
  Mentsuyu Sauce (page 6)
½ cup (120 ml) Dashi Stock
  (page 5)

DIRECTIONS

1. To make soft-poached eggs: Put each egg into a small pan or heatproof bowl. Slowly add boiling water to each bowl. Cover, and leave for 10 to 12 minutes until the eggs are soft set. Drain off the water to use.

2. Cut up the avocado into bite-sized pieces, and mix with the Sauce A ingredients.

3. Cook the somen noodles in plenty of boiling water and drain. Rinse under cold running water and drain again. Arrange in serving bowls.

4. Top with the chilled Sauce B and add the avocado from Step 1, the salmon eggs, and poached egg. Top with shredded nori seaweed.

Noodles: **Cold**
Soup: **Cold**

Real Squid Somen

"Squid somen" usually refers to a dish of very finely julienned raw squid that's eaten like somen with mentsuyu or soy sauce. This is a "real" version using raw squid, and the results are amazing! Mix in all the garnishes and condiments before eating.

SERVES 2

3 bundles somen noodles,
   1⅔ oz (50 g) each
4 oz (120 g) raw squid for
   sashimi
2 myoga ginger buds
1 sudachi or lime
2 green shiso leaves
Finely chopped green scallions,
   to taste
1 teaspoon wasabi paste
1 teaspoon grated ginger
⅞ cup (100 ml) All-Purpose
   Mentsuyu Sauce (page 6)

DIRECTIONS

1. Slice the raw squid into thin ¼-inch (6-mm) strips.
2. Shred the myoga ginger buds. Cut the sudachi or lime in half.
3. Cook the somen noodles in plenty of boiling water and drain. Rinse under cold running water and drain again. Arrange in serving bowls.
4. Top the noodles with the raw squid from Step 1. Serve with the green shiso and scallions, and top with the wasabi paste and ginger. Serve the chilled mentsuyu in a separate bowl on the side, and dip the noodles and squid in it to eat.

Lemon and Lettuce Cold Somen

The sauce for this cold somen dish is based on an English-style salad I once tried when I was working with lemons from Hiroshima prefecture. It was a simple affair, combining lemons, lettuce, a little sugar and olive oil: subtly sweet, refreshing and delicious!

SERVES 2

**3 bundles somen noodles,
1⅔ oz (50 g) each**
2 lemons
½ head iceberg lettuce
Ground black pepper, to taste

SAUCE A
**½ cup (120 ml) All-Purpose
Mentsuyu Sauce (page 6)**
**½ cup (120 ml) Dashi Stock
(page 5)**

SAUCE B
2 tablespoons olive oil
1 teaspoon sugar

DIRECTIONS

1. Tear the lettuce into small pieces. Wash and drain. Peel one lemon and slice it thinly. Squeeze the juice of the other lemon into the ingredients for Sauce A. Chill.
2. Combine the ingredients for Sauce B in a large bowl. Add the lettuce and lemon.
3. Cook the somen noodles in plenty of boiling water and drain. Rinse under cold running water and drain again. Arrange in serving bowls.
4. Top the noodles with Sauce A and the Step 2 combination and add plenty of coarsely ground black pepper.

Spicy Shrimp Sauce Somen

The springy texture of the shrimp stir fried with aromatic vegetables is delicious in this somen dish. The creamy chili sauce is further thickened and intensified with a beaten egg. This is a family favorite and is often a surprise hit with kids!

SERVES 2

3 bundles somen noodles,
   1⅔ oz (50 g) each
10 medium shrimp
1 teaspoon corn or potato starch
½ small leek or onion
1-inch (2.5-cm) piece ginger
1 tablespoon vegetable oil
1 teaspoon doubanjiang
   (available at Chinese grocery
   stores)
1 tablespoon starch water
   (page 10)
1 egg
1 teaspoon sesame oil
½ packet radish sprouts, about
   2 oz or 60 g

FOR THE SAUCE

1¼ cups (300 ml) chicken stock
2 tablespoons tomato ketchup
2 tablespoons soy sauce
2 tablespoons mirin
1 teaspoon sugar

DIRECTIONS

1. Remove the shells from the shrimp and devein. Rinse under running water. Drain and dry, and dust with a little cornstarch.
2. Chop up the leek or onion and ginger finely.
3. Heat up the vegetable oil in a frying pan, and stir fry the shrimp, green onion, and ginger. When the shrimp is cooked, add the doubanjiang and stir fry a little more.
4. Add the Sauce ingredients and bring to a boil. Add the starch water and mix to thicken. Beat the egg, and mix it quickly into the Sauce.
5. Cook the somen noodles in plenty of boiling water and drain. Rinse under cold running water and drain again. Mix with the sesame oil, and arrange in serving bowls.
6. Top the noodles with the Step 4 sauce and radish sprouts.

Even plain noodles become something special with these sumptuous sauces!

Kasahara-Style Dipping Sauces with a Difference

On these two pages I've collected a selection of dipping sauces for noodles with a difference, including the sesame-walnut sauce that's so popular at my restaurant. They go well with udon, soba or somen noodles! They all keep for up to 5 days in the refrigerator.

Packed with vegetables, you don't need additional garnishes with this.

GAZPACHO-STYLE SAUCE

SERVES 2
⅔ cup (150 ml) tomato juice
½ small cucumber
¼ onion
1 garlic clove
2 tablespoons olive oil
Coarsely ground black pepper
Salt
1 tablespoon usukuchi (light-colored) soy sauce
1 tablespoon mirin

DIRECTIONS
Blend all the ingredients together in a food blender until smooth. Chill in the refrigerator.

Doubanjiang gives this a spicy accent!

SPICY SOY MILK SAUCE

SERVES 2
1 cup plus 1 tablespoon (250 ml) unsweetened soy milk
½ cup (120 ml) All-Purpose Mentsuyu Sauce (page 6)
1 teaspoon doubanjiang (spicy Chinese bean paste, availabe at Asian grocery stores)
1 teaspoon sesame oil

DIRECTIONS
Mix all the ingredients together.

This fragrant sauce is packed with aromatic ingredients.

HIYAJIRU-STYLE COLD SAUCE

SERVES 2
1 small Pacific saury himono (semi-dried fish; available at Japanese grocery stores)
3 tablespoons miso
1 myoga ginger bud
5 green shiso leaves

SAUCE A
1⅔ cups (400 ml) Dashi Stock (page 5)
1 tablespoon soy sauce
1 tablespoon mirin
5 green scallions, finely chopped

1 tablespoon roasted white sesame seeds

DIRECTIONS
1. Mince the shiso leaves and myoga ginger bud finely.
2. Cook the saury on both sides on a grill and shred. Chop up with the miso. Put into a bowl with the Sauce A ingredients and mix well.
3. Add the Step 1 ingredients, scallions and sesame seeds and mix well.

The secret to its smooth creaminess is milk!

SESAME AND WALNUT SAUCE

SERVES 2
5 oz (150 g) shelled walnuts
3 tablespoon ground sesame or tahini
1 cup plus 1 tablespoon (250 ml) All-Purpose
   Mentsuyu Sauce (page 6)
½ cup (120 ml) whole milk

DIRECTIONS
1. Put the walnuts in an unoiled frying pan, and gently roast them over low heat. Combine the mentsuyu sauce and milk.
2. Put the walnuts and sesame paste in a food blender, and add the combined liquid ingredients little by little until smooth.

When you want to enjoy the simple flavors of the noodles.

SALTED UMAMI SAUCE

SERVES 2
1⅔ cups (400 ml) water
One 4-inch (10-cm) square piece konbu seaweed for making Dashi Stock (page 5)
½ tablespoon salt
2 tablespoons mirin
1 teaspoon sugar

DIRECTIONS
Put all the ingredients in a pan and bring to a boil. Turn off the heat. When it has cooled to room temperature, strain through a sieve.

Perfect in the summer. Great for guests too.

MENTSUYU GELÉE

SERVES 2
⅞ cup (200 ml) All-Purpose Mentsuyu Sauce
   (page 6)
⅞ cup (200 ml) Dashi Stock (page 5)
15 oz (4.5 grams) leaf gelatin or 1 tablespoon
   agar-agar

DIRECTIONS
1. Put the leaf gelatin in a container, and add enough water to cover and soften it.
2. Put the mentsuyu and stock in a pan and heat. When it's slowly bubbling, add the softened gelatin and mix to dissolve. Turn off the heat. When it has cooled down to room temperature, transfer to the refrigerator and chill until set.

Noodles: **Cold**
Soup: **Cold**

White Fish Cake and Daikon Somen

This dish takes its inspiration from a chopped udon noodle dish from the Kansai region that's topped with aburaage fried tofu. The theme here is white. White kamaboko fish cakes and daikon radish are shredded, and dashi stock is poured over both. That's it! The crispy texture of the daikon radish is a nice accent.

SERVES 2

3 bundles somen noodles,
    1⅔ oz (50 g) each
½ white kamaboko fish cake
    (available at Japanese
    grocery stores)
1-inch (2.5-cm) piece daikon
    radish
5 mitsuba or flat-leaf parsley
    sprigs
1 tablespoon toasted sesame
    seeds

FOR THE SOUP
½ cup (120ml) All-Purpose
    Mentsuyu Sauce (page 6)
½ cup (120ml) Dashi Stock
    (page 5)

DIRECTIONS

1. Shred the kamaboko fish cake and the daikon radish thinly. Pull the leaves off the mitsuba or parsley. Combine the Soup ingredients and chill.

2. Cook the somen noodles in plenty of boiling water and drain. Rinse under cold running water and drain again. Arrange in serving bowls.

3. Pour the chilled Soup over the noodles. Mix up the daikon radish and kamaboko fish cake, and put on top. Sprinkle with the sesame seeds.

Chapter Four

RAMEN AND RICE NOODLES

I love ramen. To me, ramen means the soy sauce soup ramen that my parents used to take me out for in Musashikoyama, Tokyo when I was a child. The toppings were char siu pork, grilled green onions, naruto fish cake and menma, crunchy preserved bamboo shoots, all classic components of old-fashioned ramen. Everyone has a favorite ramen shop that lingers in the memory.

   This chapter is about types of noodles that originate from China and other parts of East Asia: ramen, yakisoba (lo mein), glass or cellophane noodles and more!

All About Ramen and Rice Noodles

Freshly made Chinese noodles are the most convenient. Let's master glass noodles and Korean noodles too.

Chinese noodles are wheat noodles made with an alkaline water, which makes the noodles turn a little yellow and gives them a unique texture. When it comes to these, the freshly made kind are the most convenient and versatile. Freshly boiled, you can use them for ramen or dan dan noodles. Rinse under cold water and you can use them for cold Chinese noodle dishes. The cooked noodles can also be stir fried for yakisoba (lo mein) or deep fried to make chow mein noodles easily. When you want a change of pace and a very different texture, try chewy, springy Korean naengmyeon, which you can buy at any general Asian grocery store. Rice noodles such as bifun (often called rice vermicelli or glass noodles) are a good healthy alternative, and are nice to stock in your pantry too.

THE CHINESE NOODLES I USED IN THIS BOOK

The fresh noodles I used are the ones pictured to the upper left, a crinkly type that comes in 130-gram (a bit more than 4 ounces) hanks. The crinkled noodles combine well with soup. For firm noodles cook them for 2 minutes; for in-between cook for 2 and a half minutes, and for soft noodles cook for 3 minutes. The rice vermicelli or glass noodles I use are pictures below left, and are dried and come in 150 gram (5 ounce) bundles. They are reconstituted in cold water before cooking in boiling water for 3 to 4 minutes. The Korean naengmyeon I use (right) comes in 165 gram (5½ ounce) dried bundles.

HOW TO COOK FRESH CHINESE NOODLES

 →  →  →

Loosen up the noodles with your hands before putting them in the boiling water. By exposing as much of the surface of the noodles as possible, they will have a better texture.

Bring plenty of water to a boil in a pan, and put in the noodles. Stir up the noodles using long cooking chopsticks immediately.

Cook the noodles according to the directions on the packet, depending on how firm you want the noodles to be. Drain well into a colander.

When making ramen soups, you usually put the soup in the bowl first, and then put in the noodles. If you put the noodles in first the soup may not cover the noodles well, and the noodle strands may get stuck to each other, to be careful.

Noodles: **Hot**
Soup: **Hot**

Soy Sauce Ramen with Chicken

The foundation of this ramen is a simple soy-sauce-based soup. My favorite ramens are basic and "ordinary," like this one. But to some ramen lovers, there's nothing ordinary about it. The chicken and crunchy aromatics add a clean, refreshing finish.

SERVES 2

2 hanks fresh Chinese noodles, about 4 oz (130 g) each
2 chicken tenders (about 5 oz/ 150 g)
2 myoga ginger buds
10 green shiso leaves
⅓ packet radish sprouts (about 3½ oz/100 g)
Salt, to taste
1 tablespoon sesame oil
2 slices sudachi or lime

FOR THE SOUP
2½ cups (600 ml) chicken stock
2 tablespoons usukuchi (light-colored) soy sauce
1⅓ tablespoons mirin

DIRECTIONS

1. Shred the myoga ginger and green shiso leaves. Cut the radish sprouts into 3 pieces. Combine these in a bowl filled with cold water to crispen. Drain well.
2. Remove any sinew from the chicken tenders. Add a little salt to some water in a pan and bring to a boil. Add the chicken tenders, turn off the heat and leave for 5 minutes. Drain and wipe off the moisture, shred with your hands and mix with the sesame oil.
3. Heat up the soup and ladle into serving bowls.
4. Cook the noodles in plenty of boiling water until the noodles are separate. Drain well and add to the serving bowls. Top with the Step 1 and 2 ingredients, plus the sudachi or lime slices.

Chinese Noodles with Umeboshi, Octopus and Watermelon

Hiyashichuka is a uniquely Japanese dish of cold Chinese-style noodles with various toppings served in hot weather. This version is based on a very popular dish at my main restaurant in the summer months that combines umeboshi, boiled octopus and watermelon. I love the juxtaposition of the sour-tartness of the umeboshi and the sweetness of the watermelon. On a whim, I added a little ketchup to make it even redder, and that turned out to be a stroke of genius, if I do say so myself!

SERVES 2

2 hanks fresh Chinese noodles, about 4 oz (130 g) each
4 oz (120 g) boiled octopus (available at Japanese grocery stores or at fishmongers that sell sashimi-grade fish)
10 oz (300 g) watermelon (about ¼ of a small one)
½ small or ¼ large cucumber
5 green shiso leaves
2 umeboshi

SAUCE A
⅞ cup (200 ml) chicken stock
3 tablespoons rice vinegar
1 teaspoon sugar
1 tablespoon soy sauce
1 teaspoon vegetable oil
1 tablespoon tomato ketchup

SAUCE B
1 tablespoon vegetable oil
1 teaspoon usukuchi (light-colored) soy sauce
1 teaspoon mirin
1 teaspoon rice vinegar

DIRECTIONS

1. Combine the Sauce A ingredients and chill in the refrigerator.
2. Slice the octopus into thin diagonal slices. Cut the watermelon into ¾ inch (2 cm) dice, and reserve the rind. Slice the cucumber into thin rounds. Shred the green shiso leaves, put into a bowl of cold water to crisp, and drain well.
3. Pit the umeboshi and mix the fruit with the Sauce B ingredients. Add the octopus, watermelon and cucumber and mix quickly.
4. Cook the noodles in plenty of boiling water until the noodles are separate. Drain well, rinse several times in cold water and drain well again. Arrange in serving plates.
5. Top with Sauce A, the Step 3 ingredients and the green shiso leaves. Decorate with a piece of the reserved watermelon rind.

TIPS

Cut the ingredients so they're about the same size

Octopus, watermelon and cucumber all have different textures, so it's easier to eat them if you cut them so they're all about the same size. By putting the shiso leaves briefly in water, not only can you crisp them up, you'll eliminate any bitterness they have.

Noodles: **Cold**
Soup: **Cold**

Dan Dan Tanmen

Dan dan or tan tan noodles are a spicy dish that comes from Sichuan Province, and tanmen are a type of ramen that's topped with stir-fried pork and vegetables. This is a combination of these two classics, highlighting the best features of each. The ground meat and medley of vegetables used as a topping make this a very filling dish. Finish off by adding lots of ground sesame seeds.

SERVES 2

2 hanks fresh Chinese noodles, about 4 oz (130 g) each
2 cabbage leaves
½ onion
1 medium green bell pepper
⅓ carrot
⅔ oz (20 g) zha cai (a pickled vegetable, available at Chinese grocery stores)
1 garlic clove
1 tablespoon vegetable oil
4 oz (120 g) ground pork
1 tablespoon doubanjiang (available at Chinese grocery stores)
½ bag (about 3½ oz/100 g) bean sprouts
1 tablespoon ground sesame seeds

FOR THE SOUP
2½ cups (600 ml) chicken stock
3 tablespoons sesame paste or tahini
1 teaspoon sugar
4 tablespoons mirin

DIRECTIONS

1. Chop the cabbage roughly. Slice the onion and bell pepper thinly. Cut the carrot into matchsticks.
2. Finely mince the zha cai and garlic. Combine the Soup ingredients.
3. Heat a frying pan over low heat, heat the vegetable oil and add the ground pork, zha cai, garlic and doubanjiang. Stir fry well while breaking the meat apart with the wooden spatula.
4. When the meat changes color add vegetables from Step 1 and the bean sprouts and continue stir frying. Add the Soup and bring to a boil.
5. Cook the noodles in plenty of boiling water until the noodles are separate. Drain well and arrange in serving bowls. Pour the Step 4 ingredients over, and sprinkle with the ground sesame seeds to serve.

TIPS
Stir fry doubanjiang over low heat to bring out its fragrance

Doubanjiang is a spicy hot bean paste from Sichuan Province frequently used in Chinese-style dishes in Japan. When stir frying the ground pork in this dish, do so slowly over low heat with the garlic and doubanjiang to bring out its maximum flavor and fragrance. The doubanjiang's spiciness will be accentuated as well.

Noodles: **Hot**
Soup: **Hot**

Hot Pot Style Ramen

When we eat hot pots in Japan, we often add noodles at the very end as the "last course," a kind of savory dessert if you will. Ramen noodles are added frequently, and that's what inspired this recipe. The napa cabbage cooks until it's very soft; and the simple chikuwa fish sticks are a must. Add the shrimp at the very end so they'll be plump and delicious.

SERVES 2

2 hanks fresh Chinese noodles, about 4 oz (130 g) each
2 leaves napa cabbage
1 large green onion or ½ small leek
1 package enoki mushrooms, about 3½ oz (100 g)
6⅔ oz (200 g) boneless chicken thighs
4 medium fresh shrimp
1 chikuwa fish stick (available at Japanese grocery stores)
1 small bunch shungiku (chysanthemum greens, available at Asian grocery stores)

FOR THE SOUP

2½ cups (600 ml) chicken stock
1 tablespoon dark or regular soy sauce
1 tablespoon usukuchi (light-colored) soy sauce
2 tablespoons mirin

DIRECTIONS

1. Divide the leaves from the stems of the napa cabbage, and cut the stem parts into 2 inch (5 cm) wide strips. Chop up the leaves roughly. Slice the green onion or leek thinly diagonally. Cut the root ends off the enoki mushrooms and pull the mushrooms apart. Cut the chicken into bite-sized pieces. Remove the shells from the shrimp; devein and rinse. Slice the chikuwa fish stick into ⅓ inch (1 cm) wide diagonal pieces.

2. Heat the Soup ingredients in a pan. When it comes to a boil, add all the ingredients from Step 1, except for the shrimp, and simmer.

3. When the chicken changes color, add the shrimp and simmer briefly.

4. Cook the noodles in plenty of boiling water until they separate. Drain well and arrange in serving bowls. Pour the Step 3 soup over, and top with the ingredients, with an eye to presentation. Then add the chrysanthemum greens and serve.

TIPS

The umami is the key

By adding both vegetables and soy sauce to the stock, the soup will be deeply flavored and packed with umami.

Noodles: **Hot**
Soup: **Hot**

Noodles: **Hot**
Soup: **Hot**

Ramen with Boiled Eggs and Lotus Root Dipping Sauce

This dipping-style ramen is eaten by dipping the noodles into a miso-flavored dashi base sauce thickened with grated lotus root. The texture of the mushrooms and the sweetness of the onion are accents too. You can boil the eggs to your desired degree of doneness. Here I've soft-boiled them and crushed them into the sauce.

SERVES 2

2 hanks fresh Chinese noodles, about 4 oz (130 g) each
2 eggs
1 small section lotus root, about 6 oz (200 g)
¼ onion
1 packet shimeji mushrooms, about 3½ oz (100 g)
1 tablespoon sesame oil
2 sprigs mitsuba or flat-leaf parsley

FOR THE SAUCE
2½ cups (600 ml) chicken stock
3 tablespoons miso
2 tablespoons soy sauce
2 tablespoons mirin

DIRECTIONS

1. Make the soft-boiled eggs. Bring water to a boil in a pan and add the eggs, and boil for 5 minutes. Drain and put into cold water. Peel.
2. Peel and grate the lotus root. Slice the onion thinly. Shred the shimeji mushrooms apart. Cut the mitsuba into 1 inch (2.5 cm) long pieces. Mix the Sauce ingredients together.
3. Heat the sesame oil in a frying pan and stir fry the onion and shimeji mushrooms. When they're wilted, add the Sauce ingredients and bring to a boil.
4. Add the grated lotus root to the Sauce, and mix until it's thickened. Add the mitsuba or parsley.
5. Cook the noodles in plenty of boiling water until they separate. Drain well and arrange on serving plates. Cut the eggs in half and put on the plates. Serve the Step 4 sauce in a separate bowl, and dip the noodles in the sauce to eat.

Chilled Rice Vermicelli with Mentaiko

I took inspiration for this recipe from a dish of chilled glass noodles with caviar that I had once in a Chinese restaurant. The only additional ingredient is the mentaiko, spicy pollack roe. Combined with a generous amount of oil to mix well with the rice noodles, they become moist and delicious. This works well as an appetizer or as a light main meal.

SERVES 2

3 oz (90 g) dried thin glass or cellophane noodles
1 large piece mentaiko, about 3½ oz (100 g)
5 scallions, chopped
Shredded nori seaweed, to taste

FOR THE SAUCE

2 tablespoons vegetable oil
1 teaspoon usukuchi (light-colored) soy sauce
1 teaspoon mirin

DIRECTIONS

1. Soak the glass noodles in cold water for a while until softened. Drain well, and cut into easy-to-eat lengths. Bring plenty of water to a boil, and boil the noodles for 3 to 4 minutes and drain. Chill in ice water, and drain well again.
2. Peel the membrane off the mentaiko and mash the rest into a paste. Put into a large bowl with the Sauce ingredients and mix.
3. Combine the noodles, the Sauce and the scallions and mix well. Arrange on serving plates and top with the shredded nori.

TIPS

Reconstitute the glass noodles in water before boiling them

If you take the extra step of soaking the noodles in water before cooking them, they'll retain their texture better and flavors will infuse them more deeply as well. Moist and delicious every time!

Grated Carrot and Squid Panfried Noodles

When you grow up, yakisoba or panfried noodles become an appetizer you eat with drinks. I've loved yakisoba forever, but I am not too fond of the type with lots of additional ingredients. So here I tried stir frying some grated carrot. It becomes moist and sweet, coating the noodles nicely.

SERVES 2

2 hanks fresh Chinese noodles, about 4 oz (130 g) each
1 fresh surume squid or other type of medium squid
1 large green onion or ½ small leek
A few springs of mizuna greens (about 1 oz/30 g)
1 medium or ¾ large carrot (6⅔ oz/200 g)
2 tablespoons vegetable oil
1 tablespoon roasted sesame seeds

FOR THE SAUCE

2 tablespoons sake
1 tablespoon soy sauce
1 tablespoon oyster sauce
Coarsely ground black pepper, to taste

DIRECTIONS

1. Pull the tentacles out of the squid, and remove the intestinal organs. Pull the plastic-like skeleton out, cut in half and slice into 1 inch (2.5cm) wide strips. Cut the tentacles into easy to eat pieces. Cut the green onion into thin diagonal slices, and cut up the mizuna greens into 2 inch (5 cm) long pieces. Grate the carrot. Mince the ginger. Combine the sauce ingredients in a bowl.
2. Cook the noodles in plenty of boiling water until the noodles are separate. Drain well.
3. Heat up the vegetable oil in a frying pan and stir fry the squid and ginger. When the pan is fragrant add the green onion or leek, mizuna greens, and grated carrot and stir fry rapidly.
4. Add the boiled noodles and stir fry quickly. When the carrot has coated the noodles add the sauce, mix quickly, arrange in serving plates and sprinkle on the sesame seeds.

Chinese Noodles with Daikon Sauce

Boiled Chinese noodles are panfried on both sides to make them crispy, like chow mein noodles. The sauce is a double-punch of grated and soft-cooked daikon radish. It will really warm you up!

SERVES 2

2 hanks fresh Chinese noodles,
   about 4 oz (130 g) each
½ medium daikon radish
2 tablespoons starch water
   (page 10)
2 tablespoons vegetable oil
Coarsely ground black pepper,
   to taste

FOR THE SAUCE
2½ cups (600 ml) chicken stock
1 tablespoon usukuchi (light-
   colored) soy sauce
½ teaspoon salt
2 tablespoons mirin

DIRECTIONS

1. Peel and grate ⅓ of the daikon radish. Cut up the rest into thin, 2 inch (5 cm) wide strips.

2. Cook the noodles in plenty of boiling water until the noodles are separate. Drain well. Mix with 1 tablespoon of the vegetable oil.

3. Spread the noodles out in a frying pan, and pan fry until crispy on both sides, taking care not to burn it. Take out of the frying pan and arrange on service plates.

4. Heat up the rest of the vegetable oil in the same frying pan and stir fry the cut up daikon radish. When it is wilted add the sauce ingredients and heat through. Add the starch water and mix rapidly to thicken the sauce. Add in the grated daikon radish.

5. Pour the sauce over the noodles, and sprinkle with coarsely ground black pepper to taste.

Noodles: **Cold**
Soup: **Cold**

Somen-Style Naengmyeon

Since I have a restaurant in Seoul too, I go there quite a lot. I thought the texture of the local naengmyeon was very interesting, so here I've used it in a chilled somen-like dish. The sauce and the additions are staight-up traditional-style somen. Fun, isn't it?

SERVES 2

2 hanks fresh Korean naengmyeon, about 5.8 oz
   (165 g) each
2 eggs
A pinch salt
A pinch sugar
1 tablespoon vegetable oil
4 fresh shiitake mushrooms
2 myoga ginger buds
½ of the white part of a small leek
½ packet radish sprouts, about
   3½ oz (100 g)
1-inch (2.5-cm) piece ginger

FOR THE SAUCE
½ cup (120 ml) All-Purpose
   Mentsuyu Sauce (page 6)
½ cup (120 ml) Dashi Stock
   (page 5)

DIRECTIONS

1. Make 2 shredded egg crepes. Beat the eggs in the bowl, add the salt and sugar and mix. Heat the vegetable oil in a frying pan and pour half the egg mixture in. When the edges start to curl up, take the pan off the heat, and turn the crepe over to cook quickly. Take the crepe out of the pan, let cool and cut into thin strips. Make another egg crepe in the same way.
2. Slice the shiitake mushrooms thinly, put into a pan with the Sauce ingredients, and simmer until there's no liquid in the pan.
3. Shred the myoga ginger. Cut the leek into 2 inch (5 cm) long pieces. Shred the rest finely, and put into a bowl of cold water to crisp up. Drain well. Cut the radish sprouts into 2 inch (5 cm) pieces. Grate the ginger.
4. Cook the naengmyeon noodles in plenty of boiling water, following the instructions on the packet. Drain well, and rinse in cold running water. Drain again.
5. Put the noodles in serving bowls, add the Step 1, Step 2 and all the Step 3 ingredients except for the ginger. Put the ment-suyu and ginger in separate small bowls, and dip the noodles in the sauce to eat.

Noodles with Manila Clams and Tofu in a Thick Sauce

Be sure to coat the tofu pieces with the starch to thicken them before adding them in, so they don't get too crumbly. When the tofu has absorbed the umami from the clams, they taste so good! Add a final accent of black pepper.

SERVES 2

2 hanks fresh Chinese noodles, about 4 oz (130 g) each
1 large onion
10 oz (300 g) Manila or littleneck clams
Salt, for soaking the clams
1 tablespoon vegetable oil
2 tablespoons starch water (page 10)
1 block silken tofu, about 10 oz (300 g)
5 green scallions, chopped
Ground black pepper, to taste

FOR THE SOUP
2½ cups (600 ml) water
2 x 2 inch (5 x 5 cm) piece konbu seaweed
2 tablespoons sake
2 tablespoons soy sauce
1 teaspoon sugar

DIRECTIONS

1. Finely chop the onion.
2. Soak the clams in salt water to de-grit them. Rub the shells together to wash them, then put them in a pan with the soup ingredients and bring to a boil, When the clams open up, skim off any scum and strain the soup through a sieve to separate the liquid from the clams. Remove the clam meat from the shells.
3. Heat up the vegetable oil in a frying pan and stir fry the onion. When it's fragrant, add the Soup from Step 2 and bring to a boil. Add the starch water and stir to thicken.
4. Roughly crumble the tofu into the soup, and bring to a boil. Add the clams and heat through.
5. Cook the noodles in plenty of boiling water until the noodles are separate. Drain well and arrange in serving plates. Pour the Step 4 soup over the noodles. Top with the chopped scallions and sprinkle with coarsely ground black pepper to taste.

Chapter Five

WHEN ONLY PASTA WILL DO

Pasta uses wheat flour as its base. That means it goes well with a wide range of ingredients. We don't serve pasta in our restaurants, but for this chapter I've created eight recipes for "Japanese-style" versions, or the type made by professionally trained Japanese chefs.

Green Shiso, Butter and Bacon Pasta

I love basil, but for a Japanese-flavored pasta, basil isn't necessarily the right fit. That's when I remembered what they do at a certain well-established Italian restaurant in Roppongi, Tokyo. Apparently, when they first opened, they used to add green shiso leaves to basil, since the latter was still very exotic in Japan. The refreshing fragrance of green shiso goes so well here with the umami of bacon!

SERVES 2

5 to 6 oz (150 to 180 g) spaghetti
4 slices bacon
10 green shiso leaves (available at Japanese grocery stores, or grow your own)
1 tablespoon (20 g) butter
Salt
Coarsely ground black pepper, to taste

DIRECTIONS

1. Slice the bacon into ⅓ inch (1 cm) strips. Chop up the shiso leaves coarsely.
2. Bring plenty of water to a boil in a pan, and add 1% of its weight in salt to it. Cook the spaghetti following the directions on the packet.
3. Heat up the butter in a frying pan, and sauté the bacon.
4. Drain the cooked spaghetti and add to the frying pan with the green shiso leaves. Mix rapidly, and adjust the seasoning with salt.
5. Arrange on plates, and sprinkle with lots of black pepper.

TIPS

Salt the boiling water for pasta

Unlike Japanese noodles, Italian pasta does not have any salt in the dough. Think of the boiling water as another source of seasoning, and be sure to salt it well, with 1% of the weight of the water in salt. That means for every 2 liters or about 8½ cups of water, you will need 20 grams or 1⅓ tablespoons of salt. If you're not sure, just taste the water, and if it seems salty enough for you, it probably is right.

TIPS

Don't sauté the ingredients; just mix them together

Once you add the boiled pasta to the frying pan, don't sauté it! Simply shake the pan back and forth and mix it up quickly to combine the ingredients.

Fettucine with Chicken and Burdock Root Cream Sauce

Wide noodles like fettucine go well with creamy sauces. Chicken and burdock root is a classic combination in washoku, and the burdock root's texture provides a nice accent.

4 oz (120 g) dried fettucine
5 oz (150 g) boneless chicken thigh meat
½ burdock root
1 tablespoon (20 g) butter
Salt
2 tablespoons grated Parmesan cheese
Finely chopped green scallions, to taste
Ground black pepper, to taste

FOR THE SAUCE
4 tablespoons heavy cream
2 teaspoons soy sauce
2 teaspoons mirin

DIRECTIONS

1. Cut the chicken into bite-sized diagonally cut pieces. Cut the burdock root as if you were sharpening a pencil by running a knife repeatedly on the end of it to produce shavings. Put the burdock root shavings in a bowl of cold water and rinse briefly. Drain well.

2. Cook the fettucine in plenty of salted water. Cook for the length of time indicated on the packet.

3. Heat the butter in a frying pan and add the Step 1 ingredients. Sprinkle with salt and stir fry. When the burdock root has wilted, add the Sauce ingredients.

4. Drain the fettucine and add to the frying pan. Mix quickly, and sprinkle in the grated cheese.

5. Arrange on serving plates, topped with the chopped scallion and black pepper.

Fermented Fish and Sprout Pasta

This dish is more like a small-plate treat or drinking appetizer than traditional plate of dinner pasta! The crispy bean sprouts and spicy radish sprouts mixed with the richly flavored shuto (fermented, preserved fish) really bring your taste buds to life.

5 to 6 oz (150 to 180 g) spaghetti
⅓ package radish sprouts, about 3½ oz (100 g)
Salt
1 bag bean sprouts, about 7 oz (200 g)
3 tablespoons shuto (available in jars at well-stocked Japanese grocery stores)
1 tablespoon toasted sesame seeds
1 tablespoon sesame oil

DIRECTIONS

1. Cut the radish sprouts in half.
2. Bring plenty of salted water to a boil in a pan. Cook the spaghetti following the directions on the package. One minute before the spaghetti's done, add the bean sprouts to the cooking water.
3. Drain the spaghetti and bean sprouts and arrange on serving plates. Top with the shuto and sesame seeds. Drizzle on the sesame oil. Mix well before eating.

TIPS

Add the sprouts to the pasta

You can cook the two together. Just drop in the bean sprouts at the last minute, to give them a quick blanch. Pull everything off and drain it to retain that hint of crunch. There's nothing like it!

Garlic Chive Carbonara

I based this carbonara on the classic stir-fried dish called niratama: garlic chives with soft scrambled eggs. The key to a creamy sauce is to mix all the sauce ingredients beforehand, and to turn the heat off immediately after adding them to the pan.

SERVES 2

5 to 6 oz (150 to 180 g) spaghetti
4 slices bacon
⅓ bundle garlic chives, about 1 oz (30 g)
Salt
1 tablespoon (20 g) butter
Ground black pepper, to taste

FOR THE SAUCE
2 egg yolks
2 tablespoons heavy cream
1 tablespoon grated cheese

DIRECTIONS

1. Cut the bacon into ⅓ inch (1 cm) strips. Cut up a little of the garlic chives into ⅙ inch (5 mm) pieces, and the rest into 2 inch (5 cm) pieces. Combine the Sauce ingredients in a bowl.
2. Bring plenty of salted water to a boil in a pan. Cook the spaghetti following the directions on the package.
3. Heat the butter in a frying pan and stir fry the bacon and the longer pieces of the garlic chives. Drain the spaghetti and add to the pan, mixing rapidly. Add the Sauce ingredients and immediately take the pan off the heat. Toss to keep cooking the Sauce in the residual heat. Taste and adjust the seasoning with salt.
4. Transfer to serving plates, and sprinkle with the small pieces of garlic chives and the black pepper to serve.

Nori Seaweed and Scallops with Yuzu Kosho Pasta

Cooked nori seaweed and scallops go so well together. A small amount of yuzu kosho, the spicy citrusy condiment from Kyushu, is added. Yuzu kosho does not lose its fragrance or flavor if it is heated, so it's great for Japanese-flavored pasta dishes. Just be careful not to add too much of it though.

SERVES 2

5 to 6 oz (150 to 180 g) spaghetti
1 large green onion or ½ small leek
1 sheet nori seaweed
1 small can scallops, about 2 oz (80 g)
1 tablespoon vegetable oil
1 tablespoon sake
1 teaspoon soy sauce
½ teaspoon yuzu kosho

DIRECTIONS

1. Cut the green onion or leek into thin diagonal slices. Rip up the nori seaweed with your hands.
2. Bring plenty of salted water to a boil in a pan. Cook the spaghetti following the directions on the package.
3. Heat the vegetable oil in a frying pan and stir fry the green onion or leek. When it's wilted, add the can of scallops with its liquid and mix quickly. Add the soy sauce, sake and the yuzu kosho and mix.
4. Drain the cooked spaghetti and add to the pan. Add the nori seaweed and mix rapidly.

White Miso, Tomato and Mushroom Penne

Tomatoes and nameko mushrooms are standard pairings in hearty miso soups served in some regions of Japan. Here I 've used penne instead of the suiton (wheat dumplings) that are used in such concoctions, and made a pasta dish with a creamy white miso-tomato sauce. The mouthfeel of the nameko is great in this. Give it a try!

SERVES 2

4 oz (120 g) penne
1 medium tomato
1-inch (2.5-cm) piece ginger
½ bag nameko mushrooms,
   about 1⅔ oz (50 g, available at
   Japanese grocery stores)
1 tablespoon vegetable oil
Finely chopped scallions, to taste
Ground black pepper, to taste

FOR THE SAUCE
2 tablespoons white miso
2 tablespoons milk

DIRECTIONS

1. Chop up the tomato roughly, and mince the ginger. Blanch the nameko mushrooms quickly in boiling water and drain well. Combine the Sauce ingredients in a bowl.

2. Bring plenty of salted water to a boil in a pan. Cook the spaghetti following the directions on the package.

3. Heat the vegetable oil in a frying pan and stir fry the tomato, ginger and nameko mushrooms. When it's fragrant, add the Sauce ingredients and mix quickly.

4. Drain the pasta and add to the pan. Mix rapidly, and arrange on serving plates. Garnish with the scallions and black pepper.

Salted Salmon and Celery Aglio e Olio Pasta

I thought that the salmon I used might not be salty enough, so I added a drizzle of soy sauce at the end, which deepened the flavor and added a nutty fragrance. If you can't find salted salmon, see the Notes for instructions for making your own.

SERVES 2

5 to 6 oz (150 to 180 g) spaghetti
1 celery stalk
1 garlic clove
1 piece salted salmon, about
    3½ oz (100 g, available at
    Japanese grocery stores or
    see Notes)
Salt
1 tablespoon vegetable oil
1 teaspoon soy sauce
Coarsely ground black pepper,
    to taste
1 small red chili pepper, optional

DIRECTIONS

1. Slice the celery thinly, and mince the garlic. Cut the calyx off the chili pepper and remove the seeds.
2. Remove the skin from the salted salmon and chop up roughly.
3. Bring plenty of salted water to a boil in a pan. Cook the spaghetti following the directions on the package.
4. Heat the vegetable oil in a frying pan and add the salmon. Stir fry with a wooden spatula while breaking up the fish. When it's cooked, add the ingredients from Step 1. When everything is fragrant, add the soy sauce and black pepper.
5. Add the drained spaghetti and mix rapidly. Serve topped with the red chili, if desired.

NOTES *To make your own salted salmon: Liberally salt a piece of fresh salmon on both sides. Wrap loosely in paper towels, and put on a colander or rack. Refrigerate at least overnight, or up to 3 days. Change the paper towels if it gets soggy.*

Chilled Cappellini with Cucumber, Kiwi and Sweet Shrimp

Sweet shrimp (amaebi) are used a lot in Japanese cooking, such as sushi. Combined with the sourness of kiwi fruit and mixed with grated cucumber, the shrimp here are given a distinctive Japanese taste with wasabi. The jade green color of this dish is so pretty, don't you think?

SERVES 2

3½ oz (100 g) cappellini/angel
    hair pasta
1 small or ½ large cucumber
2 tablespoons vegetable oil
½ teaspoon salt
½ teaspoon wasabi paste
1 kiwi fruit
2⅔ oz (80 g) sashimi-grade
    sweet shrimp
Salt, for pasta water

DIRECTIONS

1. Grate the cucumber, peel and all, and squeeze out lightly. Combine with the vegetable oil, salt and wasabi paste.
2. Peel and cut the kiwi into ⅓ inch (1 cm) dice. Peel the shrimp and sprinkle with a little salt.
3. Bring plenty of salted water to a boil in a pan. Cook the cappellini following the directions on the package. Drain well and then immerse in ice water to cool. Drain well again.
4. Put the cucumber, kiwi and shrimp in a bowl and mix well. Add the chilled pasta and mix. Adjust the seasoning if need be.

Appetizers That Go Well With Noodles

When I was trying to come up with ideas for side dishes or appetizers that go well with noodles, I thought of the sides that are served at ramen restaurants. The selection of appetizers here can be eaten on the side, or you can just dump them on the noodles if you like. All of them can be made in no time.

Mashed Nagaimo Yam Salad

A creamy texture with a gentle sweetness from the cheese.

SERVES 2

12-inch (7.5-cm) piece nagaimo yam
1⅔ oz (50 g) mascarpone cheese
Salt to cook the yam, plus additional salt
½ teaspoon wasabi paste
3 scallions, finely chopped
Shredded nori seaweed, to taste

DIRECTIONS

1. Peel and cut up the nagaimo yam into bite-sized pieces. Boil in salted water until tender. Drain, and mash up roughly using a fork. Add a little salt, the wasabi paste and mascarpone cheese to the yams and mix.
2. Arrange on a serving plate and top with the green scallions and nori seaweed.

Quick Panfried Gyoza Disks

No need to fold and wrap the gyoza! Fry both sides to a crispy finish.

MAKES 10

2 cabbage leaves
5 garlic chives
⅓ small leek or large green
    onion
1-inch (2.5-cm) piece ginger
4 oz (120 g) ground pork
1 tablespoon soy sauce
½ tablespoon mirin
½ tablespoon sesame oil
20 gyoza skins
1 tablespoon vegetable oil
Japanese mustard paste (or
    English mustard powder
    reconstituted with water to
    a paste)

FOR THE SAUCE
1 tablespoon soy sauce
2 teaspoons rice vinegar
1 teaspoon chili oil

DIRECTIONS

1. Finely mince the cabbage, sprinkle with salt, and squeeze repeatedly with your hands until wilted. Squeeze out the excess moisture. Finely mince the garlic chives, leek or green onion, and ginger.
2. Put the ground pork, the Step 1 ingredients and the soy sauce, mirin and sesame oil in a bowl and mix well.
3. Dab a little water round the perimeter of each gyoza skin, and put ⅒ th of the Step 2 pork mixture on 10 of them. Top each skin with a second skin, and press down on the edges to seal them and form them into discs.
4. Heat the vegetable oil in a frying pan and put in the gyoza discs. Pan fry on both sides until crispy. Arrange on serving plates with the Sauce and mustard paste.

Cabbage and Bacon Frittata

Steam-fry this over low heat and enjoy the soft and fluffy texture.

MAKES 10

¼ small cabbage, about 2 cups
5 green shiso leaves
2 slices bacon
3 eggs
Salt, to taste
Ground black pepper, to taste
Vegetable oil, for cooking
Mayonnaise

DIRECTIONS

1. Shred the cabbage, and chop up the shiso leaves. Cut the bacon into ⅓ inch (1 cm) strips.
2. Break the eggs into a bowl. Add the Step 1 ingredients, season with salt and pepper, and mix well.
3. Heat up the vegetable oil over low in a frying pan. Add the Step 2 mixture, cover with a lid and leave to steam-fry for 5 to 6 minutes until set. Cut into 6 wedges, arrange on a serving plate and serve with a dollop of mayonnaise on the side.

Daikon Radish with Anchovies

The crispy crunchiness of the daikon radish and the saltiness of the anchovies go together perfectly. Who'd have thought?

SERVES 2

2-inch (5-cm) piece daikon radish
½ packet radish sprouts, about
    3½ oz (100 g)
3 anchovy filets
Ground black pepper, to taste

DIRECTIONS

1. Peel the daikon radish and shred finely. Cut the radish sprouts in half. Chop up the anchovies roughly.
2. Combine all in a bowl, and add plenty of black pepper.

Mushroom and Bamboo Shoot Stir Fry

Menma is a dried and fermented bamboo shoot condiment. Its crunchy texture is the key to this stir fry, which works well as a ramen topping too!

SERVES 2

½ large green onion
1 packet shimeji mushrooms,
    about 3½ oz (100 g)
1 packet enoki mushrooms,
    about 3½ oz (100 g)
1 teaspoon sesame oil
3½ oz (100 g) menma
Ichimi togashari, to taste

FOR THE SAUCE
1 tablespoon sake
1 tablespoon soy sauce
1 tablespoon mirin

DIRECTIONS

1. Cut the green onion into thin diagonal slices. Remove the roots, and rip apart the shimeji and enoki mushrooms. Combine the Sauce ingredients.
2. Heat the sesame oil in a frying pan and stir fry the onion, mushrooms and menma. When everything is wilted, add the Sauce ingredients and stir fry quickly. Add some ichimi togarashi.

Wakame Seaweed and Lettuce Salad with Kimchi

A refreshingly spicy salad with sesame oil as the accent.

SERVES 2

1 oz (30 g) wakame seaweed
    packed in salt
¼ head iceberg lettuce
1⅔ oz (50 g) kimchi

FOR THE DRESSING
1 tablespoon sesame oil
1 tablespoon rice vinegar
½ tablespoon soy sauce
1 egg yolk
1 tablespoon toasted sesame
    seeds

DIRECTIONS

1. Rinse the salt off the wakame and soak in water. Drain and squeeze out well. Rip up the lettuce with your hands. Roughly chop up the kimchi.
2. Put all the ingredients, including the Dressing ingredients, in a bowl and mix well.
3. Arrange on a serving plate. Beat the egg yolk lightly and drizzle it over the salad. Sprinkle with sesame seeds.

NOTES *If you can't find salt-packed wakame, use 3 teaspoons of dried wakame and reconstitute it in water. Drain well before proceeding.*

Chapter Six

HOT POTS AND NOODLES FOR A CROWD

Japanese-style hot pots continue to grow in popularity the world over. The donabe, or earthenware pot, that's sometimes used is the perfect vessel for the steamy, simmering and savory flavors to meld. It's comfort food at its finest and the ideal choice for a family meal or a winter weekend feast.

Somen Hot Pot

I first had this when I was invited to the home of a somen maker in Shimabara, Nagasaki prefecture. I was so impressed at how simple and tasty it was. This is eaten in the winter, when everyone surrounds a big donabe and eats freshly boiled, piping-hot somen. It's simply dipped in equally hot mentsuyu, and you quickly find you can't stop slurping up mouthful after mouthful of this appealing dish.

SERVES 5

5 bundles somen, about 1⅔ oz (50 g)
3½-inch (8-cm) piece daikon radish
¼ napa cabbage
6⅔ oz (200 g) thinly sliced pork belly
1 tablespoon sesame oil
Ichimi togashari, to taste (ground red chili pepper, available at Japanese grocery stores and by mail order)
Finely chopped green scallions, to taste
⅓ oz (10 g) katsuobushi (bonito or skipjack tuna flakes)
⅞ cup (200ml) All-Purpose Mentsuyu Sauce (page 6)

FOR THE SAUCE
1 tablespoon sake
1 tablespoon soy sauce
1 tablespoon mirin
1 teaspoon sugar

DIRECTIONS

1. Grate the daikon radish. Divide the napa cabbage into the leaves and stems. Slice the stems and roughly chop the leaves. Cut the pork into bite-sized pieces. Combine the Sauce ingredients in a bowl.
2. Heat the sesame oil in a frying pan and stir fry the pork. When the meat changes color, add the Sauce ingredients and mix quickly. Add the ichimi togarashi.
3. Bring plenty of water to a boil in a large earthware or cast iron pot and add the napa cabbage and somen noodles. When the noodles are done, scoop them out and eat them dipped in hot mentsuyu. Add grated daikon radish, katsuobushi, the pork and the scallions to your mentsuyu, to taste.

TIPS

Add umami to pork

By using spicy and sweet-salty ingredients as an addition to your pork dishes, the umami in the dipping sauces pairs perfectly. It's the same case with bentos too.

Sukiyaki Udon

Udon noodles are usually added at the end of a sukiyaki meal as the last starchy, filling course. Here they're added from the start and simmered along with all the other ingredients. Items are taken out of the pot as soon as they're cooked, and eaten with creamy beaten raw egg. The udon, packed with the umami of the meat and vegetables, is salty-sweet, soft and delicious, making this a favorite hot pot for many!

SERVES 4

3 to 4 portions frozen udon noodles, 4 oz (120 g) each
1 block (about 10 oz/300 g) yakidofu or grilled tofu (available at Japanese grocery stores)
1 small leek or 2 large green onions
4 fresh shiitake mushrooms
1 packet enoki mushrooms, about 3½ oz (100 g)
10 oz (300 g) beef, thinly sliced for sukiyaki (available at Japanese grocery stores or ask your butcher)
½ bundle (about 2½ oz/75 g) chrysanthemum greens (available at Japanese grocery stores)
4 eggs

FOR THE SAUCE
⅞ cup (200 ml) mirin
²/₅ cup (100 ml) water
²/₅ cup (100 ml) sake
²/₅ cup (100 ml) soy sauce
2 tablespoons sugar
4 x 4 inch (10 x 10 cm) piece konbu seaweed

DIRECTIONS

1. Drain the tofu lightly and cut into 8 pieces. Cut the leek into thin diagonal slices. Cut the shiitake mushrooms in half. Cut the root ends off the enoki mushrooms and pull the mushrooms apart into small clumps.
2. Cook the udon noodles in plenty of boiling water, and drain well.
3. Put the Sauce ingredients in a large earthware or cast iron pot and heat. Add the beef, the Step 1 and Step 2 ingredients, and simmer.
4. Break the eggs into individual bowls and beat. Scoop out the cooked ingredients from the pot and dip into the egg to eat.

TIPS

Cook the udon noodles with the other ingredients

This hot pot differs from the usual sukiyaki because the udon noodles are cooked along with the meat and vegetables, instead of afterward. The flavors of the ingredients infuse and permeate the noodles, giving them a rich and satisfying taste.

Chicken Paitan Soup Ramen Hot Pot

"Paitan" means a stock or soup that's been simmered until it's thick, cloudy and gelatinous. The paitan here is made with chicken, the key to this hot pot. It's based on the famous mizutaki hot pots of the Hakata area of Fukuoka. It's difficult to produce a chicken paitan stock from a carcass, so here I have used chicken wings instead. It's a luxurious, somewhat time-consuming hot pot, but the rich flavors are well worth it.

SERVES 4

2 hanks fresh Chinese noodles, about 4 oz (130 g) each
16 chicken wings (the tip and the middle section)
1 small leek or 2 large green onions
¼ small cabbage
½ bunch garlic chives
3½ oz (100 g) king oyster mushrooms
Yuzu kosho, to taste

FOR THE SOUP
6¾ cups (1500 ml) water
½ cup (120 ml) sake
4 x 4 inch (10 x 10 cm) piece konbu seaweed
1 tablespoon salt
1 onion, thinly sliced

DIRECTIONS

1. Make the paitan soup. Cut the chicken wings apart so that the tips and the middle sections are separate. Put the wingtips in a pan with the Soup ingredients, and bring to a boil over high heat. Reserve the middle sections of the wings for later. (see Photo 1 below)
2. When the liquid comes to a boil, lower the heat to medium, and simmer for about 30 minutes. Turn off the heat, and bash the wingtips with a rolling pin or similar implement to crush them. Bring to a boil again, and simmer for an additional 20 minutes. (see Photo 2)
3. When the soup has turned a creamy white color, strain the contents through a colander. (see Photo 3)
4. Put the reserved chicken-wing middle sections in a frying pan skin side down, and pan fry until golden brown on both sides.
5. Cut the leek into thin diagonal slices, and roughly cut up the cabbage. Cut the garlic chives into 2 inch (5 cm) long pieces. Shred apart the king oyster mushrooms into easy-to-eat pieces.
6. Put the Step 4 and 5 ingredients into a large pot. Add the Step 3 soup, bring to a boil and simmer until cooked through.
7. Cook the noodles in plenty of boiling water until they separate. Drain well. Add to the soup and cook briefly. Eat with yuzu kosho.

①

②

③

Tempura Feast Soba

There's a saying at soba restaurants in Japan that goes, "Make the tempura flower." This means to add just enough batter to the tempura so that it doesn't fall apart when added to hot sauce or soup. When having a tempura and soba party at home, fry just as much of whatever ingredients you and your family like. My children love hot dog tempura, which becomes amazingly juicy when fried!

SERVES 4

4 bundles dried soba noodles, 4 oz (120 g) each
1 small Japanese eggplant
1 medium green bell pepper
¼ kabocha squash
4-inch (10-cm) piece of carrot
3½ oz (100 g) maitake mushrooms
4 shrimp
4 sausages or 2 hot dogs
2 chikuwa fish sticks
Grated daikon radish, to taste
Grated ginger, to taste
⅞ cup (200ml) All-Purpose Mentsuyu Sauce (page 6)
Flour, for dusting
Vegetable oil, for deep frying

FOR THE BATTER
1 egg yolk
⅔ cup (150 ml) water
3½ oz (100 g) flour

DIRECTIONS

1. Cut the eggplant in half lengthwise, and make small shallow cuts into the surface. Cut into half lengthwise again. Cut the bell peppers into quarters or eighths (if using a large one). Slice the kabocha squash thinly, and cut the carrot into thin matchsticks. Shred the maitake mushrooms apart into easy to eat clumps. Remove the shells from the shrimp, devein and rinse. Cut the sausages in half or quarter the hot dogs. (see Photo 1 below)
2. Combine the Batter ingredients and mix together lightly.
3. Dust all the ingredients in Step 1 with flour. Dip each piece into the Step 2 mix. Heat up the vegetable oil to 340ºF (170ºC) and deep fry the ingredients in 3 to 4 batches until they're crispy, and then take out of the oil and drain. When frying the carrots, hold them in bundles when you put them in the oil to make kakiage or mini-fritters. Drain all the pieces, and arrange on a platter with some grated daikon radish.
4. Boil the soba noodles in plenty of water, then drain and rinse under cold running water. Drain again and arrange on a serving platter. Serve with individual bowls of mentsuyu.

①

TIPS

Fry denser ingredients first
Start with harder ingredients, such as squash, saving softer ones, such as seafood, for the end.

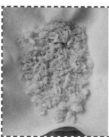

TIPS

You'll have homemade tenkasu too!
Making tempura is always a big job, but at the end you're rewarded with tasty leftovers: batter bits called tenkasu. Drain the oil well with paper towels, then wrap and freeze.

Snacks and Sides to Make with Leftover Noodles

I always tend to cook too much udon or soba, because I'm afraid of not having enough for everyone. This means that I often end up with leftovers. So I tried remaking the leftovers into drinking snacks or side dishes.

Perfect with beer!

Made with leftover glass noodles

Chilled Panfried Glass Noodles

The flavors meld together to make the perfect drinking snack.

SERVES 2

- 6⅔ oz (200 g) reconstituted glass noodles
- 4 oz (120 g) boneless chicken breast
- 2 scallions or ½ small leek
- 2 shiitake mushrooms
- 1 medium green bell pepper
- ¼ head iceberg lettuce
- 2 tablespoons vegetable oil
- Coarsely ground black pepper, to taste
- 1 tablespoon toasted sesame seeds

FOR THE SAUCE
- ½ cup (120 ml) chicken stock
- 1 tablespoon sake
- 1 tablespoon soy sauce
- 1 tablespoon mirin

DIRECTIONS

1. Cut up the glass noodles into easy-to-eat lengths. Boil in plenty of boiling water for 3 to 4 minutes and drain.
2. Cut the green onions into thin diagonal pieces. Slice the shiitake mushrooms and bell peppers thinly. Rip up the lettuce into large pieces. Cut the chicken breast in half crosswise and then into long strips with the grain of the meat. Combine the Sauce ingredients.
3. Heat the vegetable oil and stir fry the chicken. Add the green onion, shiitake mushrooms and bell peppers and stir fry.
4. Add the Sauce ingredients and stir fry until there's no liquid left in the pan.
5. Plate then chill in the refrigerator. Serve topped with black pepper and sesame seeds, with the lettuce on the side.

Made with leftover soba noodles
Deep-Fried Soba

Fry until very crisp, and eat with a squeeze of sudachi or lime.

SERVES 2

1 bundle worth of cooked soba
Vegetable oil, for deep frying
Salt
1 sudachi or lime

DIRECTIONS

1. Heat the vegetable oil to 340ºF (170ºC). Put the loosened-up soba in small bundles in the oil, and fry for 4 to 5 minutes until crispy. Drain and then arrange on plates.
2. Sprinkle with salt and serve with a sudachi or lime half.

Made with leftover somen noodles
Somen Galettes

The cooked somen makes really soft and puffy galettes.

SERVES 2

2 bundles worth of cooked somen noodles
⅔ oz (20 g) dried sakura shrimp (available at Japanese grocery stores)
5 finely minced green scallions
1 tablespoon vegetable oil
Grated daikon radish, to taste
½ cup (120 ml) All-Purpose Mentsuyu Sauce (page 6)

FOR THE BATTER
2 eggs
1 tablespoon flour
1 teaspoon sesame oil

DIRECTIONS

1. Cut up the somen noodles roughly.
2. Put the somen in a bowl, and add the sakura shrimp, the minced green scallions, and the Batter ingredients. Mix well.
3. Heat the vegetable oil in a frying pan. Divide the Step 2 mixture into 4 portions, add each portion to the pan in a 4-inch (10-cm) round. Fry on both sides until golden brown.
4. Serve with daikon radish and mentsuyu.

Made with half a portion of udon noodles
Udon Macaroni Salad

The thick, chewy udon goes so well with mayonnaise!

½ portion frozen udon noodles, cooked, about
   2 oz (60 g)
¼ onion
1 small or ½ large cucumber
Salt
1 hard-boiled egg

FOR THE DRESSING
4 tablespoons mayonnaise
¼ teaspoon Japanese mustard paste, or English
   mustard powder reconstituted with water
½ teaspoon usukuchi (light-colored) soy sauce
Coarsely ground black pepper, to taste
A pinch sugar

DIRECTIONS

1. Slice the onion thinly. Slice the cucumber thinly with the skin on. Combine with the onion and a pinch of salt. Squeeze several times, rinse under cold running water, and wring out the excess moisture. Finely chop the boiled egg. Cut up the udon noodles roughly. Combine the Dressing ingredients.
2. Combine all the ingredients in a large bowl and mix well.

TIPS

Cut up the udon before using

If you cut up udon noodles before combining them with other ingredients, the flavors will infuse them better, and the texture is macaroni-like.

Farewell and Happy Cooking!

Early in the morning before we open, when I'm in the small room in the back that I secretly call "CEO HQ" when I'm doing paperwork late at night, I can hear the sounds of noodles being slurped at the counter. I make it a personal policy not to eat meals at my restaurant, but everyone else who works there enjoys noodles all the time to keep their stomachs filled and their energy up. Soba, somen, udon, pasta: we have all types of noodles that have been featured in magazines or our TV shoots.

"Ah, noodles again today." When I hear those enthusiastic slurping sounds coming from the front, I can't help grinning to myself. Even on the busiest days of shooting or prepping for the restaurant, noodles are a treat. You can make them quickly, in quantity and be sure to be satisfied with the result.

As for myself, I tend to eat noodles late at night. After closing up at the main store, I rush over to Sanpi Ryoron for Men. I just love sipping a beer while enjoying a variety of great snacks there, and finishing up with some handmade soba noodles. (Of course it's a restaurant I created as the kind of place I'd want to go to myself, so it's natural that I should enjoy it so much!)

When I find that I've had a bit too much to drink when I'm out and about, the restaurant chain I usually seek out is Fuji Soba. Their simple warm bowl of soba noodles with a simple, delicious soup goes down so easily, and it always saves me.

Noodles are such a great food. For lunch or dinner or even for breakfast. Whether we're busy or can't be bothered to do much, noodles always come to our rescue.

—**Masahiro Kasahara**

"Books to Span the East and West"

Tuttle Publishing was founded in 1832 in the small New England town of Rutland, Vermont [USA]. Our core values remain as strong today as they were then—to publish best-in-class books which bring people together one page at a time. In 1948, we established a publishing office in Japan—and Tuttle is now a leader in publishing English-language books about the arts, languages and cultures of Asia. The world has become a much smaller place today and Asia's economic and cultural influence has grown. Yet the need for meaningful dialogue and information about this diverse region has never been greater. Over the past seven decades, Tuttle has published thousands of books on subjects ranging from martial arts and paper crafts to language learning and literature—and our talented authors, illustrators, designers and photographers have won many prestigious awards. We welcome you to explore the wealth of information available on Asia at **www.tuttlepublishing.com.**

Published by Tuttle Publishing, an imprint of Periplus Editions (HK) Ltd.

www.tuttlepublishing.com

KASAHARA MASAHIRO NO MENDO DAKARA MEN NI SHIYO
Copyright © Masahiro Kasahara 2015
Photography: Hidetoshi Hara

English translation rights arranged with SHUFUNOTOMO CO., LTD through Japan UNI Agency, Inc., Tokyo

Library of Congress Cataloging-in-Publication Data in process
ISBN 978 4 8053 1681 8

English Translation © 2022 Periplus Editions (HK) Ltd.

Distributed by

North America, Latin America & Europe
Tuttle Publishing
364 Innovation Drive
North Clarendon, VT 05759-9436 U.S.A.
Tel: 1 (802) 773-8930
Fax: 1 (802) 773-6993
info@tuttlepublishing.com
www.tuttlepublishing.com

Japan
Tuttle Publishing
Yaekari Building 3rd Floor
5-4-12 Osaki Shinagawa-ku, Tokyo 141 0032
Tel: (81) 3 5437-0171
Fax: (81) 3 5437-0755
sales@tuttle.co.jp
www.tuttle.co.jp

Asia Pacific
Berkeley Books Pte. Ltd.
3 Kallang Sector, #04-01, Singapore 349278
Tel: (65) 67412178
Fax: (65) 67412179
inquiries@periplus.com.sg
www.tuttlepublishing.com

25 24 23 22   10 9 8 7 6 5 4 3 2 1
Printed in Malaysia   2111TO